Corporate Leadership Selection

Impact on American Business, Employees, and Society

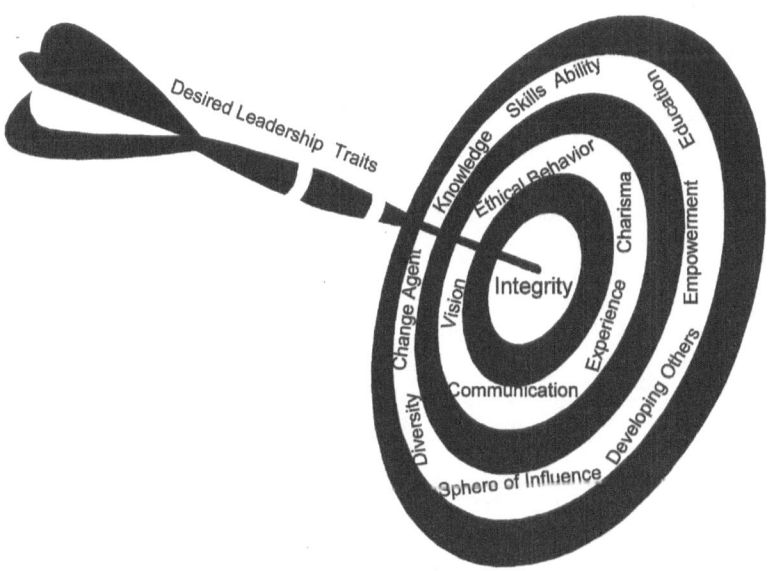

Dr. Reginald J. Gardner Jr. DM

authorHOUSE®

AuthorHouse™
1663 Liberty Drive, Suite 200
Bloomington, IN 47403
www.authorhouse.com
Phone: 1-800-839-8640

First published by AuthorHouse 12/29/2008

ISBN: 978-1-4389-4264-3 (sc)

Printed in the United States of America
Bloomington, Indiana

This book is printed on acid-free paper.

This book is dedicated to the home team –
Elise, Kevon, and Kyle.
No journey is too great with the right team,
tools, and temperament.

Preface

After 30 years of service as an executive, consultant, and vendor, I strongly believe there is a story to be told based on my observations and first-hand experiences around the evolution of corporate leader selection and its effect on the American landscape. The intent of this book is three-fold. First, I want to share my years of qualitative, phenomenological research on the topic of criteria for CEO selection in U.S. for-profit firms. Second, I want to uncover leadership behaviors in selecting other leadership and management levels in the corporation. Third, I want to provide a glimpse of the impact to American business (i.e. its employees; its vendors; and its competitors) and American society as a result of corporate leadership selection.

This book is an unbiased account of events in numerous business scenarios that I have either researched, observed, or experienced. The objective is **_not_** to paint a negative picture of corporate life and its challenges. Rather, this book will reflect upon leadership selection decisions, and the consequences (both positive and negative) of those decisions.

I am hopeful the excerpts in this book will touch the conscious of those who willingly contributed to unethical/immoral corporate leadership behavior; strike a nerve in those who have the moral courage to blow the whistle on their observed corporate wrongdoing; and open the hearts of those who will encounter questionable leadership activity in the future to respond and curtail such events. As a result, this book is geared toward existing corporate leaders; newly selected corporate leaders; those who aspire to be corporate leaders; and students who study and research corporate leader selection. The U.S. is the greatest country in the world. It is fueled by successful American corporations. However, like any other entity or process, there is always room for improvement.

Acknowledgements

Completing this book, the doctoral curriculum, and the dissertation research study was a journey that required contributions from my heart, mind, and soul. The journey involved dedication, time, and money at the expense of other long-standing personal commitments. I am extremely appreciative of the assistance I received and those who contributed to my personal development in accomplishing my goal.

I thank my family who holds the key to my heart. My wife, Elise, my sons Kevon and Kyle, my father Reginald, my mother Carlyne, my stepfather Donzell, my sister Arvella, and my stepbrother Anthony provided encouragement during this endeav-

or. They pushed my motivation buttons, oftentimes, without knowing it.

I acknowledge my doctoral research committee who challenged my mind to find the appropriate research methods and techniques to complete the research study. My committee chair, Dr. Raj Singh, and my committee members, Dr. Lee Gremillion, and Dr. Doug LePelley offered valuable feedback to my research project and Chapter Two of this book. In addition, they increased my knowledge of organizational management and leadership concepts and guided me through the research approval process.

Prior to beginning my doctoral curriculum, I completed the Kellogg School of Management Executive Education program. I was fortunate to expand my academic and real-world knowledge through four management and organizational leadership courses. I attended a *Soul of Leadership* course taught by the renowned Dr. Deepak Chopra. In a 30-minute one-on-one conversation over lunch with Dr. Chopra, I gained a true appreciation of his concept that every experience has a memory which subsequently creates a desire; and with reflective inquiry, there is no problem that can not be solved. In the *Reinventing Leadership* course taught by Dr. Pierre Casse, Associate Dean at the Business School of the University of Aix-en-Provence (France), I confirmed the notion of how crucial motivated employees are to organization effectiveness and success. I also learned about two key leadership issues from Dr. Pierre's global perspective:

first, employees are afraid to speak up when observing corporate wrongdoing because they feel it is too risky; and second, corporations are still not using their wealth of technology as effectively as they could. In the *Negotiation Strategies for Managers* course taught by Dr. Leigh Thompson, I learned sound techniques for influencing others and reaching consensus to achieve results with both those I have authority over and those I do not. Finally, I attended the *Minority Director Development Program* facilitated by Mr. Jim Lowry, Vice President, Boston Consulting Group; Dr. Donald Jacobs, Dean Emeritus Kellogg School of Management; and Professor Steven Rogers, Clinical Professor of Finance and Management. This course focused on corporate board of director selection and highlighted the lack of women and minorities on corporate boards. The course was instrumental in building my network of professionals affiliated with the Center for Creative Leadership. Mr. Lowry's passion towards equity in leadership also extends past the corporate world into the political world. Through my involvement in this course, I had the distinct honor of having a 15-minute conversation on two different occasions with an articulate, driven politician running for the Illinois Senate, Mr. Barack Obama.

I owe my existence to God Almighty, who owns my soul. My creator has given me the spiritual inspiration to take on this journey; surrounded me with a support system of family and friends to make the proper adjustments on this road to academic and social achievement; and blessed me with the strength to complete it. I am forever grateful.

About the Author

Dr. Reginald Gardner is a senior business executive with a proven and distinguished track record in successful delivery of business solutions – predominantly through the use of information technology. Dr. Gardner has served in a leadership capacity in Fortune 500 Companies in the insurance, oil, and retail industries. He has an extensive background of accomplishments in Leadership, Business Transformation, Information Technology, Project Management, Resource Management, and Research.

In the corporate environment, Dr. Gardner has developed and implemented project management offices; managed application development, quality assurance, and production support teams. In addition, Dr. Gardner has managed outsource service providers and third party vendors' operations. He has negotiated outsource service provider contracts in excess of $1 Billion. Further, Dr. Gardner has worked as an advisory services consultant in two reputable and successful technology consulting firms.

Academically, Dr. Gardner received his doctoral degree in Management and Organizational Leadership from the University of Phoenix. He holds an MBA from Lewis University in Human Resource Management; and a Bachelor of Science degree in Business Administration from Illinois State University. In addition, Dr. Gardner is certified in Leadership and Management from the prestigious Executive Education Program at the Kellogg School of Management at Northwestern University.

Dr. Gardner is an adjunct faculty member at the University of Phoenix and at National-Louis University where he teaches Organizational Theory and Behavior; Supervision and Leadership; and Introduction to Research Utilization. He is a member of the Academy of Management. He has been a member of the Society of Human Resource Management Professionals (SHRM) and the Project Management Institute (PMI). Gardner has also been listed in the International Who's Who in Technology.

In fulfillment of corporate (and individual) social responsibility, Dr. Gardner is a lifetime member of the National Association of Black MBAs. He has served as Chapter President of Black Data Processing Associates (BDPA), a professional information technology, non-profit organization. Dr. Gardner has also served as President of the BDPA Education & Technology Foundation.

Finally, Dr. Gardner has extensively researched the topic of leadership selection, primarily at the CEO level. He has conducted qualitative research with CEOs, corporate board members, HR professionals, and executive search firm personnel involved in CEO selection. Dr. Gardner serves as Vice President and Chief Information Officer of a privately-owned luxury motor coach company.

For more information on leadership selection criteria, leadership selection impact, or phenomenological research, you may contact Dr. Gardner at doct06@email.phoenix.edu.

TABLE OF CONTENTS

Chapter 1:
Introduction

The Current State

During the past ten years, there have been an infinite number of books written on leadership. For every book written, there has been either a new definition of what leadership is, or support for an existing definition of what leadership is. Extensive research has been conducted on leadership selection, leadership results, and the effectiveness of leadership decision-making.

Since 1999, institutions of higher education have either established or enhanced their executive education program and business school curriculum to specifically address the need for sound business leadership. On an annual basis, there are leadership conferences, forums, and seminars with leading researchers in the area of leadership, management, and organizational development. In today's technology-based environment, there are blogs, journals, newsletters, and webinars used for delivering and learning leadership techniques.

Despite the energy exerted, once-highly successful companies across the corporate landscape in multiple industries have struggled, downsized, merged, and failed since 2000. Corporate acquisitions, corporate takeovers, bankruptcies, bailouts, stock devaluations, and reports of unethical corporate practices dominate the business headlines. The firm's leaders (and their actions, attitudes, and behaviors) are the lynchpin to corporate success. Prior leadership experience, leadership development, and instinct are solid requirements for corporate leaders to have, but integrity, honesty, and sound corporate citizenship are traits that have forged to the forefront in today's business environment.

However, there is a shortage of leaders who fulfill all of the basic expectations that employees, vendors, shareholders, and customers look for in corporate leadership. Charan, Drotter, and Neal (2001) suggested filling the corporate pipeline with talented leaders in an ever-changing business environment is part of the challenge in helping companies remain successful. Charan et al (2001) also pointed out the reduced investment in talent development. In an effort to cut costs, corporations are quick to dramatically decrease or totally eliminate leadership training and development initiatives. Moreover, highly talented leaders often change jobs. Thus, retaining competent leadership is difficult. Additional discussion on filling the corporate pipeline can be found in Chapter Three.

Another sign of the current state of the corporate landscape are the U.S. Department of Labor statistics. According to Fox (2008), the outplacement firm Challenger, Gray, and Christmas reported 75,000 layoffs in January 2008. Within a five-year period, this was over a 69% increase in reported monthly layoff statistics. Although the housing and financial sectors were hit hard, other industries such as the automotive, retail, and technical services also realized significant layoffs. It is important to note that U.S. Department of Labor statistics on unemployment only reports layoffs of documented cases. There are additional unemployed and displaced Americans that are not included in the U.S. Department of Labor statistics. Arguably, these layoffs can be attributed to leadership decision-making on how to deal with managing increased corporate operational costs. Leaders must be able to identify and adapt to changes in their business environment. Too often in today's environment, adaptability translates into layoffs.

RECOGNIZED SUCCESSES

Although there have been a number of failures and missteps, there are also examples of successfully-run companies. There are six companies listed here that have navigated the ups and downs of their marketplace and consistently excelled above their competition. These companies have been successful over extended periods, and have awards, happy stockholders, proud employees and satisfied customers to prove it. They have withstood the test of time.

The Malcolm Baldrige National Quality Award was created by Public Law 100-107, and signed into law by the U.S. Congress on August 20, 1987 (Latham & Vinyard, 2004). This award highlights performance excellence through three competencies; Strategic Leadership; Execution Excellence; and Organizational Learning. Applicants must describe their corporate capabilities in 37 areas. It is an intensive undertaking, and winning the award just once is a significant accomplishment. Two of the six successful companies identified in this chapter have won the Malcolm Baldrige Award twice!

Boeing Corporation Aerospace Division received the award in the service category in 2003. The Boeing Corporation Airlift & Tanker Division received the award in the manufacturing category in 1998. The Dana Corporation Spicer Driveshaft Division received the award in the manufacturing category in 2000. The Dana Corporation Commercial Credit Division received the award in the service category in 1996.

The remaining four companies are also well known. In the banking and investment industry, Wells Fargo has maintained its stock valuation, corporate reputation, and integrity while other banking and investment firms have faltered. Please note that this book was written while the leadership of the U.S. government discussed a $700+ billion bailout of prominent, prestigious investment and loan companies.

In the airline industry, Southwest Airlines remains highly successful and profitable in their market. At times, they are ridiculed; and at times they are emulated for their low-cost operating approach. Yet, it appears that employees, investors, and customers are content with their corporate approach. Moreover, Southwest Airlines was recognized as one of the most admired airlines in the industry (Fortune, 2006).

Rue and Byars (2007) singled out Southwest Airlines in an example of servant leadership. According to Rue and Byars (2007), servant leadership is based on the idea that the leader exists to meet the needs of the people they lead. Immediately following the September 11, 2001 terrorist attacks, Southwest Airlines gave their employees hourly updates to keep everyone informed of what was happening. At that time, there were over 35,000 Southwest Airlines employees. The top three leaders of the company chose to work without pay for the remainder of 2001. Further, the company committed to no layoffs and reduction in their service schedule. In an effort to demonstrate its commitment to its staff, the company also placed nearly $200 million into the employee profit sharing plan. My research did not uncover any similar examples of servant leadership and employee commitment of this magnitude.

Exxon Mobil has reported over $35 billion in profits for 2006 and 2007. The oil industry has been extremely profitable. However, Exxon Mobil exceeds its competitors in profitability. While consistently making record profits, Exxon Mobile leadership does not hesitate to demonstrate its commitment to corporate social responsibility. CSR Wire (2008), the corporate social responsibility newswire, reported Exxon Mobil committed $10 million to New Orleans schools after Hurricane Katrina in 2006; $100 million to Stanford University's Global Climate and Energy Project in 2002; and $16 million in support of higher education as part of the largest educational matching program in the country in 2000.

Finally, Wal-Mart has been consistently successful, reporting corporate revenues of over $200 billion annually. During the past ten years, Wal-Mart has been the leader in the retail industry. In some form or fashion, Wal-Mart's operations are researched and analyzed in business classes throughout the nation. Specifically, the Wal-Mart approach to managing costs, vendor relations, and workforce diversity are of major interest.

In the context of sound leadership, the executives in these companies have successfully led their organizations. However, recognition here does not imply these companies do not have leadership challenges. In addition, there are undoubtedly other highly successful corporations. There are also extremely competent and passionate leaders in other companies that are executing (or developing) turnaround strategies to improve productivity and enhance the company reputation. These six were merely chosen to highlight their accomplishments in some of the troubled industries in American business, and to provide a glimpse of the impact of selecting good corporate leadership.

EVOLUTION OF BUSINESS ORGANIZATION AND LEADERSHIP

To have an understanding of the current state of business organization, and leadership in general, it is beneficial to review its evolution. According to Jones (2007), business organization and leadership can be traced back to the Stone Age. The earliest forms of organized business were tribes and clan's members. Survival was dependent upon cooperation. Only by organization, teamwork, and communication could tribes sustain themselves and thrive. There was organization through divisions of labor (hunters; food gatherers; craftspeople; cooks, etc.). There was teamwork and cooperation to bring down "big game" or to combat other tribes. There was communication (probably open and honest communication) on accomplishing a common goal – survival.

From the Stone Age, business evolved to feudalism, mercantilism, and capitalism. During feudalism, one class of people controlled all the resources – land, property, and people. The class in control with all of the authority was known as aristocrats.

The business form known as mercantilism was depicted as a system where products were exchanged across markets and countries until they were consumed in the market where they created the most value and use. The key to effective mercantilism was access to other countries and markets. This is somewhat similar to our modern day concept of globalization, of course on a much smaller scale.

The next evolution of business organization Jones (2007) described was the Industrial Revolution. Businesses in this era prospered from enhancements in production and trade through technological advancements – specifically the steam engine. This innovation also paved the way for other successful industries of its time such as coal mining, railroad, and cross-country transportation (both business and personal).

From the Industrial Revolution rose the form of business organization near and dear to our hearts, known as Capitalism. This system allows "ordinary" people to own resources and engage in the commerce of goods and services. Unfortunately, the growth and success of capitalism also gave rise to workplace conflicts in leading employees.

Along with the start of business organization in the Stone Age, a form of power and authority was developed to manage goal-directed activity. Jones (2007) highlighted four phases in the hierarchy of authority. First, there was ranking people according to their relative rights and responsibilities to control and use resources. Second, based on hierarchical level, one has the right to make decisions and the right to expect obedience from those below them in the hierarchy. Third, ranking in the hierarchy would change if/when one demonstrated the ability to effectively use resources for the benefit of the organization and its members. Fourth, those in decision-making positions also bear the responsibility as to whether or not their decisions work as planned.

Regardless of how business has changed, there were always two factors to drive success. One, there were innovations and technological advancements that improved worker productivity and organization effectiveness (i.e. fire, the wheel, the steam engine, mass production, computers). Two, those with the ability to adapt, embrace, and effectively use the technological advancements were placed in the leadership roles of their organization (with the possible exception of the concept of birthright or inheritance where one may be "born" into the leadership role).

After reviewing the basic elements of business organization evolution, it is apparent that somehow, somewhere our current business environment has lost its way. The concepts of integrity, loyalty, trust, teamwork, and honest communication have been pushed to the side and replaced with instant (personal) gratification, displaced accountability, and the corporate bottom line – not annual valuation, but on a monthly/quarterly basis! Moreover, one's demographics have more influence on pay, promotion, and prosperity in the corporation than productivity, performance, and potential. Leaders at all levels of the organization have a role to play and the opportunity to enhance the company reputation and employee perception by their attitude and behavior. The following chapters will attempt to analyze processes used to select leaders and briefly discuss the social and financial implications of those selection decisions.

Chapter 2:
From The Top -
Criteria For Ceo Selection

Research Study Background

During my doctoral program, I conducted a research study which explored criteria used for CEO selection in for-profit U.S. corporations. The study reviewed past CEO selections in for-profit corporations since the year 2000 to identify trends in CEO selections. This research study also highlighted potential CEO selection criteria for leading U.S. corporations in today's diverse, technology-based, global economy. The study investigated and attempted to answer the question, "What are the criteria for CEO selection in U.S. for-profit companies?"

The study also provided an overview of the importance and societal impact of CEO selection. It focused on the general problem in CEO selection of CEO turnover; the specific challenges of criteria used for CEO selection in that technology expertise is not considered in an era where technology is vital to corporate success; and the qualitative, phenomenological research method used to conduct the study. Further, the study delivered a theoretical framework that described issues and controversies in the area of CEO selection criteria.

The Chief Executive Officer (CEO) role in U.S. for-profit corporations is unique. Khurana (1998) emphasized that unlike other executive positions who report to a single individual, the CEO reports to a group of individuals – the board of directors. CEO dismissal and selection goes beyond impacting the company's internal stakeholders. The CEO sphere of influence affects a firm's shareholders, suppliers, and customers as well.

The criteria for CEO selection vary from company to company. Hollenbeck (2002) contended that CEO selection is a reflection of the organization's identity. Charismatic leadership, transformational leadership, business acumen, and a steady progression of roles with increased profit and loss responsibility and complexity are key traits that boards seek in CEO candidates (Charan, 2005; Kaplan, 2006; Khurana, 2002).

Purpose and Significance of the Study

According to Charan (2005), CEO turnover is increasing. In 1995, the average CEO tenure was 9.5 years. In 2005, the average CEO tenure was 7.6 years. Concerns over financial performance, corporate governance, leadership integrity, and stockholder confidence place corporate board members in a position of closely monitoring corporate operations. Corporate valuation fluctuates, shareholders become disgruntled, and corporate boards cope with CEO dismissal pressures (Rhim, Peluchette & Inam, 2006).

Auchterlonie (2003) quoted a study conducted by Booz Allen Hamilton which reported involuntary CEO successions increased from 2001 to 2002 by more than 70%. "The problem isn't just that more CEOs are being replaced. The problem is many CEOs are being replaced badly" (Charan, 2005, p. 74). CEO tenure is getting shorter which results in more frequent CEO hiring.

Charan (2005) wrote, "Almost half of the companies with revenue greater than $500 million have no meaningful CEO succession plan" (p.74). Due to the lack of succession planning and development, internal candidates do not receive the right experiences and testing. When no comprehensive succession plans are in place, corporations select external CEO candidates. In 2003, 55% of outside CEOs who departed were forced to resign by their boards (Charan, 2005).

This qualitative, phenomenological research study examined criteria used for CEO selection and explored trends in the CEO selection process. The study focused on for-profit companies based in the United States. The general population group analyzed was the corporate board of directors, HR personnel, and executive search firm leaders who participated in CEO selection criteria development and the CEO selection process.

The purpose of this study was to review past CEO selection criteria, and examine current CEO selection criteria trends. The study's purpose was to also provide insight into future CEO selection criteria corporate boards will consider based on changing environmental conditions such as: technological advances; workplace demographics; and market globalization. Creswell (2003) stated phenomenological research helps identify human experiences relating to a phenomenon. Leedy and Ormrod (2001) further defined phenomenology as one's perceived meaning of an event.

Corporate boards are under more scrutiny and are defined by their ability to select a good CEO (Graziano & Luporini, 2003). A phenomenological research study was appropriate and helped identify themes and patterns in CEO selection criteria as described by Creswell (2002), as well as facilitated interviews with decision-makers involved in the CEO selection process to understand their experiences. In addition, the phenomenological design helped to obtain data about individual and collective interpretations and meanings of CEO selection criteria without imposed, pre-conceptions about CEO selection criteria (Coldwell, 2007). Finally, the phenomenological research design offered CEO selection criteria alternatives in the hope of generating a new paradigm based on identified and interpreted trends (Turner, 2005).

The specific population group for this study was corporate board of directors (both past and present board members) involved in the CEO selection process. HR personnel and executive search firm leaders involved in the CEO selection process were also studied. Data for the study was collected from semi-structured interviews with 12 executives from the specific population group.

Corporate operations in 2007 are distinct from corporate operations prior to the year 2000. King (2001) stated the CEO role has become more complex and more difficult to fill. Technology advances, workplace diversity, globalization, and corporate governance are now key factors along with corporate valuation, corporate productivity, and shareholder expectations. This study was significant because it took into consideration prior research and observations of CEO selection criteria as well as introduced new industry challenges – specifically technological advancement. The study also examined technical expertise as an essential component of CEO selection criteria.

Board members involved in the CEO selection process will benefit from this study. The study highlighted the importance of technological leadership in today's technology-based, global economy. Using technology to monitor security and manage risk is critical in today's corporate landscape (Day, Gunther & Schoemaker, 2000).

With technology come unanticipated and unpredictable outcomes (i.e. computer malfunctions, power outages, inappropriate access to data, identity theft). According to CIO Insight (2006), organizational risk and security strategies should be combined. Today's technology innovation is considered a risk because a negative outcome can prevent execution of normal company operations. Technical innovation is a security factor because an abnormal stoppage may result in non-compliance of regulated policy (CIO Insight, 2006). This study is significant to leadership because it highlighted the importance of vision around the use of technology, and the potential of technical expertise as a larger component of CEO selection criteria.

Extensive literature exists on CEO selection. Numerous studies have been done to observe CEO selection and analyze corporate performance as a result of the selection (Brockmann, Hoffman & Dawley, 2006; Fisman et al, 2006; Jones, 2006; Rhim et al, 2006). This research study conducted personal, in-depth interviews with corporate board of director decision-makers, corporate HR personnel, and executive search firm personnel who participated in the CEO selection process.

Using qualitative research strategies in this study yielded substantive data to create new and different meanings for organizational, communal, and systemic societal change (Etchegary,

2006). The qualitative research method facilitated interviews and discussions on CEO selection criteria with those involved in the process. Creswell (2003) cautioned important distinctions can be made as the understanding of a phenomenon advances. As an example, the criteria for CEO selection in a company may change while the CEO recruiting and selection process is in place.

Turner (2005) suggested qualitative research is used to explore information, inquire about processes, and generate theories based on data. Qualitative research is also used if the problem relates to what is occurring. This qualitative research study helped examine research participants' experiences with CEO selection criteria as the dynamics of the business environment changed.

A pure quantitative, statistical driven approach was ruled out for this study. Moustakas (1994) stated studies of human experiences can not be explained through quantitative methods. Qualitative research seeks meanings of experiences rather than measurements. Qualitative research obtains descriptions of the experience by first-hand accounts in conversations and interviews with those who experienced the event. In addition, qualitative research helps to formulate questions and problems that reflect interest, involvement, and personal commitment of those conducting the research (p.21). A qualitative research method was used, and face-to-face personal interviews were conducted to examine experiences of decision-makers involved in developing and reviewing CEO selection criteria.

This study used a phenomenological research design. Groenewald (2004) acknowledged the German philosopher Edmund Husserl (1859 – 1938) as a leader of phenomenological research. According to Groenewald (2004), Husserl believed people can be certain about how things appear in their own consciousness. In order to arrive at certainty, anything outside of immediate experience must be ignored (p. 4).

Phenomenology was an appropriate research design because it reviewed past events and behavioral trends of those who experienced the phenomenon. Moustakas (1994) depicted phenomenology as a human science research approach that obtains data from participants' experiences through open-ended questions, and describes the experience based on the interpretation of the participants' story. The objective of phenomenological research is to determine what the experience of the event means for the people who had the experience.

As an example, Ocasio (1999) conducted a quantitative study of 120 U.S. industrial companies and explored the reliance on formal and informal corporate governance rules and their effect on CEO succession. He believed that boards of directors make decisions based on historical precedents and formal, institutionalized rules that do not readily change. Ocasio (1999) viewed organizational rules as applied procedures in the enactment of social studies. He found that rules are embodied in the organization's policies, programs, and procedures. The older the organization, the more difficult to change behavior and beliefs becomes. The selected methodology design facilitated board member interviews, reflection upon board member experiences, and perceptions on corporate institutionalized rules and technology leadership in CEO selection criteria.

The Research Question

The research study's guiding research question was: "What are the criteria for CEO selection in U.S. for-profit firms?" The criteria and the process for CEO selection vary for each company. No two organizations consider the same issues (or the same process) the same way (Hollenbeck, 2002; Southerland & Mackey-Ross, 2006). Through qualitative research, this study posed a series of questions to research participants in order to identify themes in CEO criteria and selection.

Respondents were asked questions in an effort to substantiate (or refute) the existing literature on CEO selection criteria. Research showed that corporate boards seek charisma more than they seek candidates who fit the organizational culture (Bennis & O'Toole, 2000; Khurana, 2002; Muller, 2004). Magnusson and Boggs (2006) posited that international experience is a defining factor in CEO selection.

Townsend (1996) found that performance, image, and exposure helped female executives advance. Hadlock, Lee, and Parrino (2002) discovered that CEOs in electric and gas firms have less-prestigious educational backgrounds, but more legal and regulatory expertise. Walker and LaRocco (2004) stated personal qualities of integrity, honesty, and trust is now very important. Credibility and honesty are essential leadership foundations (Kouzes & Posner, 2002).

Al-Alsheikh (2001) analyzed the differences in research studies that viewed CEO succession as a process or as an event. He found that CEO candidates' characteristics will be different from those of their predecessor, but will be similar to board members involved in CEO selection. Researchers who view CEO succession as an event pose questions around the subsequent organizational performance (Cannella & Shen, 2001; Davidson, Nemec & Worrell, 2001). Researchers who view CEO succession as a process pose questions around employee development and succession planning (Zajac & Westphal, 1996). Asking for a comparison of CEO traits discerned the theme of driving significant corporate change, or maintaining the status quo.

Contingency theory suggested CEO dismissal and CEO successor choice is predicated on corporate performance (Brockmann et al, 2006). Increased demands from institutional investors place continuous pressure on corporate boards for exceptional leadership and improved management practices (Farrell & Whidbee, 2002; Plitch, 2003). Rhim et al (2006) investigated 209 CEO successions and the association between successor and subsequent performance. Rhim et al

(2006) found investors react favorably to CEO turnover announcements, and the announcement of CEO turnover implies change is being made to improve corporate performance.

"Boards should have a clear methodology for choosing a CEO, one that operates while the CEO is firmly in place and slides smoothly into gear when the CEO leaves office" (King, 2005, p.6). Curry (2005) emphasized that getting the right players into the "C level" positions and developing them is just as important as the CEO succession planning process. Unanticipated events may lead to CEO departure. When an unanticipated event occurs, the board must have a pipeline of candidates to choose from.

Charan (2005) examined a study done by the Corporate Leadership Council human resource research organization. The research showed that in a survey of 276 large companies in 2004, only 45 (or 20%) of responding human resource executives were satisfied with their top-management succession processes. Charan (2005) suggested internal CEO succession occurs in companies that have a meaningful succession planning process already in place. Chartrand (2005) stated succession planning processes from prior years were masked to prevent employees not identified as high potential from becoming unmotivated. Now, organizations inform employees and senior leaders exactly where they stand.

Wiersema (2002) observed board members do not always have a detailed understanding of the corporation's problems and needs. As a result, the board can only give executive search firms vague advice and criteria for recruiting CEO candidates. Further, boards pay a great deal of attention to pleasing the investment community. Instructions and criteria given to executive search firms call for high-profile, charismatic leaders rather than for someone who can lead the company (Bennis & O'Toole, 2000; Charan, 2005; Khurana, 2002).

The steps taken in the CEO selection process vary. Southerland & Mackey-Ross (2006) recommended a basic approach towards CEO selection: establish a search committee; select a search firm; assess organizational needs; identify and evaluate viable candidates; check candidate references; and extend an offer to the finalist. Scrutinizing the board itself, mutually agreeing on CEO expectations, and measuring soft qualities (i.e. integrity, honesty, developing others) should also be considered in the process (Bennis & O'Toole, 2000; Vancil, 1987). Whatever format used, the board members involved in the process must possess the skills to conduct in-depth interviews with CEO candidates (Thompson & Thompson, 2003).

Organizational use of technology can provide a benefit and competitive advantage (Day et al, 2000; Katz, 2003). However, technology can also provide uncertainty and significant risks. Organizational risk and security strategies must be integrated into the corporation's overall goals and objectives (CIO Insight, 2006).

Day et al (2000) suggested that technology can provide a competitive advantage, but that advantage often goes to the companies that are most adept at choosing and implementing technological options. Day et al (2000) went on to state that some organizations risk technology uncertainties for the benefit of a competitive or personal gain. Corporate leaders should have an understanding of the sociotechnical systems that are part of the organization's core processes and their effect on organization performance (Katz, 2003).

Ben-Megachim and Gelbard (2002) explained that information technology has become a large part of the overall corporate budget. Technology expenses are high and must be monitored. The corporation's solvency may hinge on its strategic use of technology. Today's corporate leader should have an understanding of how the introduction of innovation and technology may impact the existing environment.

Ives (2004) found that by understanding and utilizing technology advances, U.S. corporations are moving technology and service jobs abroad and fueling market globalization. McCarthy (2002) cited a study by Forrester Research that estimated 3.3 million jobs would move from the U.S. to other countries by 2015. Senior leadership in large companies have identified off-shoring as a viable strategy for reducing operations costs. As a result, commandeering the offshore initiative and leading a virtual, global organization may also be considered CEO selection criteria.

Theoretical Framework of CEO Selection

Succession is an opportunity for organizational members to participate in a process that may significantly shift the organization's direction (Bass & Stogdill, 1990). When CEO succession comes from the outside, the organization that supplied the successor must also find a replacement. Because of the competitive nature of today's business world, the ever-changing customer, shareholder, and employee landscape, CEO turnover and selection can be expected to continue.

As a result of the shortened CEO tenure, more developed and qualified candidates are needed. Walker and LaRocco (2004) found that corporate boards are establishing new, higher expectations regarding succession requirements, information on talent, and development plans. Further, boards are getting guidance and support from corporate human resource executives on succession and employee development while leading the process across the organization.

Researchers are divided as to what the selection criteria should entail. Researchers who found internal CEO selection as essential (Agrawal, Knoeber & Tsoulouhas, 2006; Bartlett, 2006; Chartrand, 2005; Curry, 2005; Hunte-Cox, 2004; Marsh, 2006; Spoolman, 2005; Tsoulouhas, Knoeber & Agrawal, 2007), stressed the importance of the board to be actively engaged in the corporate succession planning process. This research examined board member behavioral patterns and employee development. Researchers who found external CEO selection as essential (Dahya & McConnell, 2003; Davidson, Nemec, Worrell & Lin, 2002; Groysberg, Nanda & Nohria, 2004; Magnusson & Boggs, 2006; Muller, 2004; Totty, 2006; Wiersema, 2002), stressed the need for the board to clearly communicate to executive search firms the CEO candidate competencies.

Some research studies found neither internal nor external criteria selection, but candidates' leadership qualities as the primary element for successful CEO selection (Ciampa, 2005; Khurana, 2001; Maccoby, 2004). King (2001) wrote, "Leadership succession is a major issue, and companies that have well-developed succession plans often eclipse their competition" (p. 5). However, the CEO career path and development experiences are changing. CEO leaders must now lead an organization that contains numerous employee demographic differences. Today's organization consists of differences in:

1. Age – entry level employees from 21 years old to employees close to retirement in their early 70s;
2. Race – an American population with an increasing amount of minority (African, Asian, Hispanic, and Native American) employees;
3. Gender – an increase of qualified and talented women in the workplace;
4. Alternative life-style employees; and

5. Americans with Disabilities Act (ADA) employees.

Simultaneously, the CEO must maintain or improve the company's value to retain stockholder confidence. Biggs (2004) emphasized that serving on a board and managing CEO succession is more difficult than it was five years ago. Shaw (2005) stated defining CEO competencies are underestimated, and reiterated some practical guidance suggested by the Business Roundtable (2002) for CEO development and selection. Carver (2003) stressed the CEO role is one of performance. CEO selection criteria should also consider candidates that can provide leadership and produce results within governance polices and guidelines.

Scope and Limitations of the Study

This study examined for-profit U.S. companies that replaced their CEO between the years of 2000 and 2005. In addition, the study focused on for-profit companies with annual revenues greater than $100 million between the years of 2000 and 2005. The research study scope was defined in order to keep the study at a manageable size for conducting a comprehensive analysis, and to complete the data collection process in a timely fashion (Groenewald, 2004).

Similar to for-profit corporations, nonprofits have challenges with leadership turnover, accountability, and technology (Ahmed, 2005). Nonprofit organizations are vital and highly-respected entities. However, this phenomenological study interpreted board members' lived experiences and behaviors with external shareholder pressure and stock market reaction to CEO dismissal and CEO selection announcements. Corporate boards are influenced by financial investors. Existing literature suggested corporate boards make CEO selection decisions to appeal to financial investors (Wiersema, 2002). As a result, nonprofit organizations were outside the scope of the study.

Further, the analysis of CEO compensation was limited in this study. "Very few business topics attract as much public attention as the paychecks of top executive officers in the largest U.S. companies" (Murphy & Zabojnik, 2004, p.192). This study examined corporate board members' behavioral patterns and themes rather than CEO monetary considerations. Respondents' patterns and themes that included compensation as criteria for CEO selection were recorded and coded. However, no research questions on CEO compensation were conducted in this study.

Boyd (2001) suggested 2 to 10 participants are sufficient for a phenomenological study. Weidenbaum (2003) reported that 90% of the time, the CEO chairs the board of directors in a dual role. Board members understand what is included in CEO selection criteria from their own experiences as CEOs. This study interviewed 12 participants. A sample size of 12 corporate board members was representative of corporate boards in U.S. for-profit firms. Interviewees were qualified to represent the general population of board members because of their experience of the phenomenon from the perspective of board member and the perspective of CEO. However, the research may have under-represented behavior and perceptions of corporate board members in firms whose annual revenues were less than $100 million between the 2000 and 2005 timeframe.

The scope of the study was narrowed to explore corporate boards' attempts to appease shareholders; and identify the relevance of technology as selection criteria. The study showed bias towards directors' experiences and interactions with their company's shareholders. Lived experiences are better displayed when they relate to decisions based on human interaction with others. Board member experiences based on meeting shareholder demands may be more important and weighed higher than CEO selection based on candidates' prior performance and ability to lead the company (Khurana, 2002).

Review of Existing Literature on CEO Selection Criteria

The objective of the literature search was to identify and examine scholarly works pertaining to criteria for CEO selection, and to review other phenomenological studies in the area of CEO succession. Category searches were done looking for phrases and key words to collect resource information. The category search stayed within a range of the past 20 years, 1987 – 2007. The list of journals and documents researched included: *Acad-*

emy of Management Journal, American Economic Review, Chief Executive, CIO Magazine, Consulting Psychology Journal, Electronic Journal of Business Research Methods, Harvard Business Review, Information Management Journal, International Journal of Management, International Journal of Qualitative Methods, Ivey Business Journal, Journal of Business, Journal of Business Ethics, Journal of Corporate Finance, Journal of Management and Governance, Journal of Management Development, Journal of Managerial Issues, Journal of Private Equity, Management Review, MIT Sloan School of Management, and the Strategic Management Journal.

This was not a comprehensive, all-inclusive list of the research done. However, the list summarized the amount of research done for this study. Moreover, all of the articles, journals, dissertations, and books reviewed were not included in this study. Some of the research considered for this study was eliminated because: it was not peer-reviewed; it was written over five years ago; it did not address the criteria for CEO selection in a substantive way; or it was not aligned with the concepts of phenomenological research reflecting the lived experiences of corporate decision-makers involved in the CEO selection process. Particular interest was given to articles and studies that addressed board member experiences in: developing CEO selection criteria; interacting with corporate HR personnel to identify and groom internal CEO candidates; and/or interacting with executive search firms to collect data on external CEO candidates.

The corporation's board of directors is accountable for CEO selection in U.S. firms (Walker & LaRocco, 2004). Selecting a Chief Executive Officer is a crucial decision an organization makes. CEO selection is a reflection of the organization's identity – its culture, people, strategy and structure, and environment (Hollenbeck, 2002). Additionally, the CEO sphere of influence can significantly impact entities internal and external to the firm. CEO selection can affect the organization's employees and its stockholders. CEO selection can also affect society in general. Qing, Maruping, and Takeuchi (2006) posited CEO succession impacts organizational capabilities, human capital, and the social structure in which the organization is embedded in. Having the right person in the CEO role is important.

One of the corporate board's most important assignments is CEO selection (Hoffman, Schniederjans, & Sebora, 2004; Southerland & Mackey-Ross, 2006; Swain & Turpin, 2005). However, no one can accurately predict how an internal CEO candidate will perform at the CEO level. Nor can one predict how an external candidate's prior experiences will translate into success in the new organization. Stellar performance at one company may not translate into success at another company (Khurana, 2002).

HISTORICAL OVERVIEW OF CEO SELECTION

Research showed CEOs are educated, and in positions to influence American business (Keiser, 1995). Keiser (1995) researched some of the earliest CEO studies that were done between 1900 and 1950. He found CEOs were better educated than the public, and they tended to come from financially privileged backgrounds. Keiser's (1995) research on CEO selection from 1950 – 1980 noted CEOs' educational levels had increased to include more MBAs and business degrees, and their self-reported backgrounds were more frequently middle-class.

In today's business environment, other CEO traits are equally important but those traits may change based on the economic climate. Walker and LaRocco (2004) suggested executive skills in organization restructuring are important during difficult economic times. During the *dot com* era of the late 1990s, technical experience was critical. "Today, the personal qualities of executives are considered important. Although difficult to assess or predict in individuals, integrity, honesty, and trust are given more prominence" (Walker & LaRocco, 2004, p. 13).

Corporations are faced with the challenge of developing leaders, but corporations have not developed enough talented leaders to successfully fill the internal pipeline with CEO level candidates. Zhang (2001) researched the theory of leadership supply and demand. The supply of CEOs (and leadership in general) is less than the demand. Ample succession planning processes do not exist to ensure future leadership demands will be met. A new dynamic has arisen where boards attach succession planning to the CEO's bonus compensation to meet leadership demand (Naveen, 2006). Companies that do not have a CEO succession planning process select an external CEO candidate (King, 2001).

Charan (2005) stated much of the board's time is devoted to monitoring accounting, Sarbanes-Oxley, risk, and financial performance. Rose (2007) found that corporate directors view maximizing shareholder value as their primary goal. Corporate boards look to external search firms to handle the CEO candidate process. If the board does not reach consensus on the criteria for CEO selection, the external search firm may step in and either develop the criteria or present CEO candidates that fit the criteria external search firm recruiters feel is important.

External search firms can only be as effective as the criteria they are given for finding CEO candidates (Totty, 2006; Wiersema, 2002). The corporate board of directors must clearly articulate CEO selection criteria; first to itself and second to the other entities involved in the search (Khurana, 2001; Southerland & Mackey-Ross, 2006). Simultaneously, the board must communicate CEO criteria and work experiences internally to the corporate HR department in order to obtain assistance with the external search as well as to establish a succession planning process for the purpose of developing future leaders internally (Kesler, 2002).

From a historical perspective, Ocasio (1999) posited CEO succession in U.S. industrial companies is institutionalized and based on formal and informal corporate governance rules. According to Ocasio (1999) corporate rules empower and control the social construction of organizational practices. Further, corporate rules are not only the reflection of corporate decision-makers, but are also shaped by history and experience, and are not easily changed. In a similar analysis, Khurana (2002) conducted a study of 850 U.S. companies and found that CEO selection is culturally determined - and inefficient.

CURRENT FINDINGS ON CEO SELECTION

CEO selection is essential to corporate long-term success. "The corporate board of directors has a legal responsibility, under Security and Exchange Commission's (SEC) rules, to select the CEO and corporate officer positions" (Walker & LaRocco, 2004, p.10). Based on their understanding of the corporation's business strategy and operational requirements, the corporate board of directors is expected to put the right executives into senior management positions, including the CEO position. Depending on industry trends, changes in the marketplace and corporate vision, the criteria for successful CEO selection can (and will) change.

Chartrand (2005) maintained that succession planning is not a strategy to immediately replace people in certain positions, but a systematic process that is integrated into a strategic plan. A challenging scenario for grooming future CEOs is the fact that the internal development process can take years to complete. In the time it takes to groom an internal candidate, the market and the corporate direction or strategy may have significantly changed.

Charan (2005) suggested a company must do three things to increase the probability of successful CEO selection. First, the company must maintain a deep pool of internal candidates kept well stocked by a leadership development process. Second, the board should create, update and refine a succession plan with a process for making decisions about candidates. Third, if the board is still considering external candidates, they should lead the executive selection firm process and not allow the executive search firm processes lead them.

King (2001) used the term *crossover* CEO to describe external CEO selections from other industries. He believed that crossover CEOs from other industries are brought into an organization in order to architect a major transformation. Regardless of what term is used, the role is the same: the corporation is in need of a leadership change. The corporate board of directors believes that change is best done with an external candidate.

Bennis and O'Toole (2000) warned of the potential danger in using external search firms in the external candidate search.

Corporations are looking to fill the top leadership role in their company. Executive search firms typically have little or no expertise in evaluating leadership experience. They will have to be reminded of paying attention to a factor they may not know how to monitor.

The criteria for successful CEO selection will vary depending on the corporation, the market trends, and most important, on the things the corporate board of director selection committee feels the company needs in its chief executive (Allgood & Farrell, 2003; Datta, Guthrie & Rajagopalan, 2002; Hollenbeck, 2002; Kwak, 2002; Muller, 2004). Before being selected as CEO, candidates must first be *considered* for the CEO position. Multiple researchers have suggested the following three criteria for candidates on the CEO career path:

1. P-I-E – According to Townsend (1996), the key ingredients for career advancement can be summed up in the acronym PIE (performance, image, and exposure). Throughout their career, CEO candidates must have consistently exceeded performance expectations; developed a leadership style that other leaders are comfortable with; and sought out difficult and high visibility assignments.

2. Progression – Charan (2005) suggested the best preparation for CEOs is progression. This is done through positions with responsibility for steadily larger and more

complex profit and loss centers. Management of multi-million profit and loss ($50M - $100M) centers is essential to ensure the candidate may have reasonable success as the chief executive.

3. Personal Qualities – Walker and LaRocco (2004) stated today's business leaders' personal qualities are considered important. CEO candidates' integrity, honesty, and trust are given more prominence than in the past.

There are other criteria used for CEO selection. Khurana (2002) emphasized corporate boards seek CEO candidates with charisma and stellar performance from other companies. However, without these basic 3P's, candidates will not be considered.

In the medical industry, Kaplan (2006) found that the top, highly experienced physicians who climbed to the positions of hospital CEOs had two specific qualities. The first quality was leadership. It includes a common and well-versed list of traits such as vision, passion, effective communication and the ability to motivate others. The second quality was business acumen. Business acumen requires the ability to manage people, execute strategy, generate revenues, maximize assets, and acquire capital.

Magnusson and Boggs (2006) stressed international diversification as the most important criteria for today's leaders. Their research shows that a CEO's international experience is linked to the firm's level of internationalization. Moreover, CEO's with international experience are better able to take advantage of the benefits of international diversification than CEOs who do not have international experience. Further, CEOs with international experience are better equipped to lead the organization's global strategy.

Researchers have discovered a multitude of reasons for CEO selections:

1. Poor corporate performance (Brockmann et al, 2006: Davidson et al, 2001; Khurana, 2002; Wiersema, 2002);

2. Unexpected departure – illness or death (Behn, Dawley, Riley & Yang, 2006; Davidson, Shengui, Worrell & Rowe, 2006);

3. Shareholder pressure for leadership change (Fisman et al, 2006);

4. Board of director power and influence (Santora, 2004);

5. Shifts in corporate governance trends (Carver, 2003; Carver, 2004; Fisman et al, 2006; Hermalin, 2005);

6. Institutionalized rules (Ocasio, 1999); and

7. Well-executed succession planning (Fulmer & Conger, 2004; Garman & Stowe, 2004)

Each CEO selection scenario is different with different selection criteria. In their selection criteria, corporate boards consider organizational fit, organizational context, and situational leadership factors (Allgood & Farrell, 2003; Bass & Stogdill, 1990). Regardless of the situation, board members are most comfortable selecting CEO candidates whose demographics are similar to their own (Zajac & Westphal, 1996).

Research on CEO succession and CEO selection highlighted multiple criteria for CEO consideration (Byrne, 1999; Khurana, 2001; Wiersema, 2002; Zhang, 2001). Technology experience was listed as criteria considered for CEO selection only once (Khurana, 2001). There were even research studies that took advantage of the use of technology to create analytical techniques and computer-based models for CEO selection (Hoffman et al, 2004). However, technology was not listed as CEO selection criteria.

Opposing Viewpoints on CEO Selection Criteria

The existing literature on CEO selection criteria is divided between the choices of an internal or external CEO. Internal selection is dependent upon a comprehensive corporate succession plan and the corporate desire to maintain the status quo (Bartlett, 2006; Charan, 2005; Chartrand, 2005; Curry, 2005; Hunte-Cox, 2004; Marsh, 2006; Rothwell & Poduch, 2004; Walker & LaRocco, 2004). External selection implies a need for change (Khurana, 2002; King, 2001; Zhang, 2001). The corporate board will solicit assistance from an executive search firm to identify candidates.

Muller (2004) posited CEOs fall into one of three categories: those who focus on the status quo; those better at general change/modification; and those who work best at turnarounds or transformation. Depending on industry trends, changes in the marketplace, corporate performance, and organizational vision and objectives, the criteria for CEO selection can change during the selection process. Depending upon the corporate needs, CEO selection criteria may fit one of three categories Muller (2004) listed.

Qing et al (2006) suggested corporate boards incorporate social network considerations into their CEO selection process. CEO candidates' intrafirm and interfirm networks are important, and should align with the organization's goals at the time of succession. Wiersema (2002) emphatically stated investors' concerns drive CEO selection. Corporate stock valuations are partly driven by confidence in the CEO. Corporate boards pay attention to satisfying the investment community, and investors welcome outside CEOs who represent a change in corporate operations. The investment community welcomes the outsider, who supposedly represents a beak from the past, by temporarily pushing up the company's stock price (Wiersema, 2002, p. 4).

Internal CEO Selection

Corporations seek leaders who have already proven to be successful in roles with significant profit and loss accountability, and in roles with increased responsibility (Kaplan, 2006; Khurana & Nohria, 2002). King (2001) suggested corporate boards prefer an orderly CEO transition; hiring an outsider involves more risk in terms of familiarity than desired. Keiser (1995) maintained that when an organization's performance is satisfactory, changing strategy or direction is not needed. In this case, an internal CEO candidate may fit the criteria for selection. Internal CEO candidate selection provides consistency, stability, and familiarity (Rhim et al, 2006). However, Charan (20025) cautioned that too much familiarity may lead to complacency through critical due-diligence processes.

Vancil (1987) described two succession styles that are used in internal CEO selection. *Relay succession* occurs in anticipation of the current CEO stepping down. The organization designates a successor. The successor is groomed for the CEO role, and subsequently, assumes the role. *Horse race succession* occurs when the board identifies viable internal CEO candidates and the candidates compete for the top spot. Tsoulouhas et al (2007) stated favoring inside CEO candidates is advantageous. The contest serves as incentive and induces employees to exert effort if they are seeking the promotion to CEO. Groysberg et al (2004) suggested the best approach for executive selection is to recruit good people, develop them, and retain as many of the stars as possible. Groysberg et al (2004) maintained that homegrown talent will not only outperform imported talent, but will also be more loyal to the organization. Therefore, recruiting and developing from within enhances the expertise of future CEO candidates.

Marsh (2006) posited that the failure to develop leaders internally triggers three undesirable impacts. First, lack of internal leader development deters the executive succession process. Second, it neglects internal potential leaders. Third, it enhances the probability of the corporation lagging behind other corporations in attracting talented executives who sense minimal advancement opportunities due to lack of internal promotions to the CEO level.

Charan (2005) wrote, "Something is seriously amiss in the business of developing and hiring CEOs. Too many top leaders fail in office; too many succession pipelines are bone dry" (p. 72). He suggested internal development is best done through positions with accountability and responsibility for steadily larger and more complex profit and loss centers. Internal CEO succession can only occur successfully in companies that maintain and execute a comprehensive succession planning process. As high potential leadership candidates are identified, they must be given on the job experience that emulates the current business environment and matches the corporate vision. Further, the leadership team accountable for succession planning must monitor and evaluate each candidate's performance at each phase of development and provide feedback that will enhance the learning and development experience.

Kesler (2002) argued CEO succession fails and the corporate leadership bench never deepens because the idea of developing one's replacement is flawed. Kesler (2002) wrote, "The very notion of developing one's own replacement implies that the judgment of the incumbent leader is the best judgment" (p. 39). Kesler (2002) also stressed that limiting the leadership search to hand-picked candidates who have been mentored by the incumbent is a mistake and limits the pool of potential candidates.

External CEO Selection

The term outside CEO can have two meanings: 1) *intra-industry* which is outside of the corporation, but inside the industry the corporation operates in and; 2) *outside-industry* which is outside the corporation, and outside the industry the corporation operates in (Datta et al, 2002; Kwak, 2002, Zhang & Rajagopalan, 2003). In either case, selecting an outside CEO implies a need for corporate change in vision, strategy, or direction (Allgood & Farrell, 2003; Brockmann et al 2006: Khurana, 2001). External CEO selection is also inconsistent with any developed or planned internal succession processes (Davidson et al, 2006). When corporations do not have comprehensive succession plans in place, they select external candidates (Charan, 2005).

According to Charan (2005), approximately 37% of the Fortune 1000 companies are run by an external CEO. An outsider is typically chosen to do a corporate portfolio restructure and to turn the company around.

Crossover CEOs (King, 2001) are brought into the organization to design and lead change initiatives. In this scenario, the selection criteria consist of: transitional leadership, problem solving skills, and the ability to rectify a downward-spiraling organization in a short period. This external leader may not possess the true, transformational leadership skills to lead an organization over the long-term.

Kwak (2002) found corporate boards are looking at a larger pool of CEO candidates, both intra-industry and outside-industry. In her analysis, Kwak (2002) also observed the risk of hiring a CEO from outside the industry. Corporate boards have less information about leaders outside of the organization's industry. Nonetheless, boards are willing to take a risk in hopes of finding someone who can lead the company.

Khurana (2002) noted that struggling companies look for a new CEO that is charismatic. In a study of over 850 large U.S. companies, Khurana (2002) found that the CEO criteria of charisma and *larger-than-life* candidates are inefficient for three reasons. First, the quest and selection of charismatic leaders is ineffective because the abilities and experiences a CEO acquired from one organization may not be transferable and successful at another organization. Second, there were company-specific competencies that drove the leader's performance at their prior company (Groysberg et al, 2004; Khurana, 2002). Those competencies may not be the same at the new company. Third, defining and identifying charismatic leadership is difficult. Measuring it will be just as difficult. Paul, Costley, Howell and Dorfman (2002) defined charisma as of divine origin, exemplary, and inaccessible to the ordinary person. "How do you measure vision, inspiration, and conviction?" (Bennis & O'Toole, 2000, p.172)

Another factor observed for external CEO selection is pressure from shareholders and the demand for improved management processes and corporate performance (Davidson et al, 2002; Khurana, 2002; Muller, 2004; Ocasio, 1999; Wiersema, 2002). The corporate board is concerned with making decisions that appeal to the investment community. The board will pay more attention to pleasing investors than to ensuring the right CEO criteria and candidate is selected (Khurana, 2002; Wiersema, 2002).

Shareholder pressures impact the CEO selection. Shareholder pressure means change is needed. However, that mandate does not specify what the criteria for the change should be. Fisman et al (2006) found that shareholders' views may not always be correct. More observations on shareholders' influence are included in the discussion on corporate board responsibility on page 50.

To further support the theme of *selection of an outsider implies change*, Herrity's (2002) research found outside directors with demographic characteristics of a new CEO that differ from the characteristics of the exiting CEO. Criteria for successful CEO selection are pervasive. However, if an outsider is considered, their traits will be different from those of the incumbent (Zajac & Westphal, 1996).

When considering external CEO candidates, the board of directors must also analyze the potential fit of the candidates with the existing corporate culture. Even though external candidates are typically brought into the organization to lead a corporate transformation, the new CEO should be compatible with the corporate culture – unless the objective and strategy is to change that culture. Corporate fit is important. Hollenbeck (2002) stressed the selection of a CEO is a reflection of the organization's identity. CEO candidates should align with that corporate culture.

Muller (2004) pointed out corporate boards go through methodical processes for assessing CEO criteria and CEO selection. However, boards do not address how CEO candidates fit with the day-to-day organizational culture. Muller (2004) went on to state that societal parameters and business expectations factor into CEO selections.

Muller (2004) suggested society feeds off of short-term, immediate gratification. Further, Donaldson (2003) reiterated the fact that Corporate America has a short-term focus

— stressing the importance of quarterly earnings and potentially lucrative stock options over long-term corporate strength and performance. Corporate boards look for a leader to fill these short-term desires. Rhim et al (2006) mentioned that corporate boards frequently respond to perceived downturns in corporate performance by replacing the CEO, which only produces short-term increased corporate valuation.

Datta et al (2002) reviewed the existing staffing literature and emphasized the match between an individual's skill set and the task requirements of the position. Stevens and Ash (2001) offered the notion to analyze the match between the people and organizational attributes such as culture and management style. Datta et al (2002) went one step further and introduced a third consideration — the match between an individual and a firm's industry characteristics. The firm's industry characteristics are skills that have value to the industry but are not transferable to another industry.

Allgood and Farrell (2003) reviewed the aspect of comparing the previous CEO to the person selected as the new CEO. Their study predicted the tenure for new CEOs based on organization performance, and provided the reason for turnover of the prior CEO. For example, a poor-performance organization that dismissed the prior CEO can bring in an outside CEO and expect improved organizational performance and a longer tenure than the prior CEO. In contrast, an internal CEO successor will have difficulty in implementing change and will have a shorter tenure if the prior CEO was dismissed. This concept of match quality (Allgood & Farrell, 2003) may also serve as CEO criteria.

Executive Search Firm participation plays a role in meeting criteria external CEO selection. Charan (2005) noted executive recruiters are honest and highly professional. Yet, executive recruiters can wield disproportionate influence in CEO succession decisions. In order to ensure they receive viable external candidates with the desired characteristics, corporate boards must clearly articulate their needs to executive search firms. When a corporate board can not reach consensus on the selection criteria, executive recruiters may provide the criteria, which may not meet the organization's leadership requirements.

ALTERNATIVE VIEWPOINTS ON CEO SELECTION CRITERIA

Research showed alternative viewpoints on what characteristics are considered, and what characteristics are not considered in CEO selection. Townsend (1996) found that female executives agreed what helped them advance their position was performance, image, and exposure (PIE). Without these fundamental ingredients, a candidates' other characteristics will not be considered. Townsend (1996) further identified the fact that female executives were clustered in jobs outside the typical career path to senior leadership. Women in the executive ranks were over-represented in staff support functions such as communications, human resources, and legal affairs.

Although most literature suggested no standard CEO selection technique, Sebora and Kesner (1994) presented a CEO selection process model that they believe *is* used by corporate boards of directors. The model contains three components: aspirations, judgment, and justification. In addition, there are three factors under which the components are prioritized as valid CEO selection criteria: organization performance; qualified candidate availability; and CEO office standardization. The board of directors will limit their need for information by agreeing to an aspiration level; then they select dominant candidates from the available pool; and build a case to support their selection that will appease the corporation's fiduciary principles.

Hoffman et al (2004) developed an analytical, computer-based model for making CEO selection decisions. Their approach combines strategic management concepts, the operations research technique of goal programming, and PC technology to provide corporate boards a computer-based model for CEO selection. The model also provides a preference ordering of candidates in case the first CEO selection is not available.

In the healthcare field, Kaplan (2006) mentioned experience in operations management, executing strategy, and managing the day-to-day business is required criteria. To be considered for the CEO position, one must demonstrate they are a proficient businessperson who happens to be a physician; not a proficient physician who happens to understand business (Kaplan, 2006).

Kaplan (2006) documented the advice of eight experienced physician executives. He observed that leadership is the number one success factor for CEOs in the healthcare industry.

Hadlock et al (2002) compared CEOs of electric and gas utility firms with CEOs of unregulated firms and found no difference in CEO tenure. However, CEOs in electric and gas utility firms are more likely to have a legal background and regulatory expertise. Further, CEOs of electric and gas utility firms tend to be older and have a less-prestigious educational background.

Whether the selection is internal or external, Bartlett (2006) observed that CEO succession requires a formal plan. In a study of the Credit Union National Association, Bartlett (2006) noted that a formal CEO succession plan helps to ensure credit union member services will continue to run smoothly. In addition, a formal CEO succession plan satisfies regulators' expectations.

Takeda, Helms, Klintworth, and Sompayrac (2005) offered one final viewpoint. In a study conducted on CEO selection and Fortune 500 CEO hair color, they found only 11 CEOs had blonde hair, 17 CEOs had red hair and the remainder had either brown or black hair. According to the study, CEOs with brown or black hair are considered as better CEO choices. However, more research is needed to substantiate hair color and CEO selection criteria.

Corporate Succession Planning Processes

Walker and LaRocco (2004) viewed succession planning as *succession management*. Succession management is not about counting talent shortages, but matching talent with future requirements. Walker and LaRocco (2004) also observed that most companies have long had in place some form of succession planning processes to ensure a supply of executive talent to meet future needs. However, with today's heightened concern for effective corporate governance, companies are taking a fresh look at their current practices and are taking steps to define and meet new expectations.

In a counter position Charan (2005) stated, "Almost half of companies with revenue greater than $500 million have no meaningful CEO succession plan, according to the National Association of Corporate Directors" (2005, p. 74). Charan (2005) continued that those companies with succession plans are not happy with them. Charan (2005) pointed out a study conducted by the Corporate Leadership Council (CLC), who surveyed 276 companies in 2004 and found that only 20% of responding HR executives was satisfied with their top-management succession processes.

According to Chartrand (2005), succession planning is a strategic process of integrating personal and professional development. It consists of identifying employees who have developed or who have the potential of developing the skills to meet organizational needs. Succession planning helps to identify employees who can assume key organization positions, or who could be expected to do so with specific development. Wallin, Cameron, and Sharples (2006) also defined succession planning as a process. Organizations ensure appropriate future leadership through a talent pipeline with the capability of sustaining long-term organizational goals. Without a comprehensive succession planning process in place, "promoting from within" into the CEO position will not be successful.

CORPORATE BOARD OF DIRECTOR'S RESPONSIBILITY

The corporate board of directors is accountable for CEO selection. Walker and LaRocco (2004) maintained the role of the board of directors is to ensure the company's leadership is carrying out the company's goals and objectives. Walker and LaRocco (2004) explained the board's involvement in the CEO selection process as a defining factor of who will be chosen to lead the company in executing those goals and objectives.

There are numerous peer reviewed articles on the subject of selecting leaders (Al-Alsheikh, 2001; Byrne, 1999; Hollenbeck, 2002; Khurana, 2002; Walker & LaRocco, 2004; Zajac & Westphal, 1996). However, the research did not imply standard criteria for CEO leadership selection. Al-Alsheikh (2001) viewed the CEO succession and selection process as still in the early stages of development. In some cases, the corporation has a succession planning process in place for identifying and developing its future leaders, and the company's board of directors selects the corporation's second in command. Yet in other cases, the board of directors selects an executive search firm to find their CEO, or the board allows the outgoing CEO to select their successor.

In a study of executive-search consultants and CEO candidates, Khurana (2001) observed that corporate directors established a narrow field of candidates and those candidates are judged based on their performance in their past companies. Zhang (2001) suggested CEO selection is a matter of supply and demand. The available supply of viable CEO candidates is lower than the need for stellar, corporate leadership. Regardless of the criteria, Thompson and Thompson (2003) stated that an integral part of board members' skills must be the ability to conduct in-depth interviews and identify viable candidates that fit with the organization's culture.

CEO dismissals have brought added challenges to the CEO selection process for corporate boards. Sometimes the CEO selection results in an abrupt CEO firing. Jentner and Kanaan (2006) conducted a study of 1590 CEO turnovers from 1993 to 2001 and found CEOs are likely to be dismissed after both bad industry and bad market performance. According to Allgood and Farrell (2003), a substantial percentage of CEO turnovers occurred in the first few years of the CEO's tenure. In more quantitative terms, Sebora (1996) reported 34% of the CEO tenures in his sample ended by the CEO's fourth year.

Allgood and Farrell (2003) suggested matching the right person to the right job can be difficult. CEOs must lead the firm, appeal to shareholders, and aid the board's efforts in complying with corporate governance. Fisman, Khurana, and Rhodes-Kropf (2006) found corporate board governance as an important factor in the CEO performance and CEO firing relationship. Through the concept of job match theory, Allgood and Farrell (2003) found neither good workers nor good employers, just good job matches. In an effort to sustain a good match, some companies have brought back their retired CEOs to run the company; known as boomerang CEOs (Jones, 2003).

Addressing this problem is important because of the impact on corporate productivity when the wrong leader is selected. "The right CEO can make or break a company, yet boards go about CEO selection all wrong" (Byrne, 1999, p.2). The interview and selection process is expensive. The cost is exponential when the wrong person is selected, and subsequently, has to be replaced. When a leader is picked that does not fit in with the organization culture and is not capable of performing the required duties, subordinates' productivity also suffers.

The study of CEO selection criteria is also important because CEO successions present organizational learning and organizational adaptation opportunities. CEO selection and succession may induce knowledge transfer. Zhang and Rajagopalan (2003) found that CEO successions enhance the company's leadership processes in identifying and reacting to change. Muller (2004) cautioned the introduction of a new CEO may lead to personal and organizational chaos. The corporation's employees are representatives of the corporate history and also serve as bellwethers of future successes.

Zajac and Westphal (1996) conducted a study of 232 CEO successions in 198 industrial and services firms and compared CEO successor functional background, age, and education with that of corporate board members and the outgoing CEO. They found sociological and psychological factors influenced CEO selection. Board members are comfortable with CEO successors who resemble their own demographic background. Because of board members' diverse demographic backgrounds, the organizational balance of power helps to predict the demographic characteristics of the successor CEO.

Zajac and Westphal (1996) also discovered that boards typically make a CEO change after experiencing poor corporate performance. When the board selects an outside successor, the successor's demographics (in functional background and education) are different from the outgoing CEO, but similar to board members. Furthermore, the selection of a CEO with a similar background to board members provides the board with a greater capacity to influence the new CEO and may ease board members' uncertainty about their selection.

Maccoby (2005) emphasized the fact that corporate leadership must articulate and model organizational values. The board must operate at the highest level of integrity. They must demonstrate integrity throughout the CEO selection process. The board's decisions and activities are carried out now with close observation and a heightened degree of vigilance from the investment community and shareholders. As a result, the board must consider CEO candidates that also have a track record of high integrity in an effort to meet shareholder expectations.

The board of directors has the ultimate accountability for CEO selection. Yet, the board's level of involvement varies across companies. Walker and LaRocco (2004) identified three levels of board of director involvement in the CEO selection process; *a passive role; a reviewing role; and an active involvement role.*

A passive board of directors may review candidates for the CEO position whom are categorized through the succession process as "ready now." The talent identification and talent assessment is typically done by the existing CEO when a passive board is in place. In addition, the board pays very little attention to planning and executive development issues.

A reviewing board of directors may review CEO candidates who are categorized as "ready now" and ready within five years. A "reviewing board" of directors will not depend solely on the CEO to identify and assess talent. They will get to know CEO candidates through interaction with them. A reviewing board of directors will also analyze the next assignments and development experiences for CEO candidates in the pipeline.

An actively involved board of directors will review CEO candidates who are in strategically important positions comprising the executive leadership team, or "C" level executives. An actively involved board of directors may even participate in the talent identification and assessment through in-company visits and compare internal talent with external talent. Finally, an actively involved board of directors will participate in planning and development issues by sponsoring project teams, coaching, and mentoring CEO candidates. An actively involved board of directors will also enhance the probability of successful CEO selection.

An additional requirement for corporate boards is the ability to identify a possible emergency replacement for unanticipated losses. If a comprehensive succession planning process is in place with a pipeline of potential CEO candidates, an emergency replacement will be easier to identify. If a comprehensive succession planning process is not in place, seeking an outsider for the CEO role may increase.

Federal regulations call for corporate board of director independence (Sarbanes- Oxley Act, 2002). Board independence is defined as a board comprised of directors who do not have any personal or professional relationships with the firm, its subsidiaries or affiliates, or firm's management (Daily & Dalton, 2003). Corporate boards are currently accused of not having their finger on the pulse of the organization and not understanding the criteria for CEO succession (Graziano &

Luporini, 2003; Shaw, 2005; Wiersema, 2002). The Sarbanes-Oxley Act of 2002 may further distance the board from fully grasping the organization's criteria for solid leadership. More research will be needed to analyze this scenario.

Executive Search Firm Participation

Charan (2005) pointed out corporate boards are not fully engaged in the CEO selection process. In a research survey conducted at the University of Southern California, Charan (2005) found 40% of corporate directors called their involvement in CEO succession planning less than optimal. CEO succession typically involves a third actor, the executive search firm (Khurana, 1998).

Khurana (1998) believed executive search firms should only be used as an intermediary in a complex labor market transaction and not the primary source of information about potential candidates and their capabilities. The executive search firm intermediary role consists of three important functions:

1. Coordinator – the executive search firm draws on its experience to assist the corporate board search committee, which has limited experience with CEO searches.
2. Mediator – the executive search firm manages a process where CEO candidates and the board gain each others trust though exposure to equal levels of risk.

3. Legitimator – the executive search firm provides an aura of professionalism that *legitimizes* the process.

Bennis and O'Toole (2000) believed the corporate board must first reach consensus on a shared definition of leadership. Executive recruiters can only be as successful as the information and the criteria they are given for CEO selection. Without clear direction from the corporate board, executive recruiters provide CEO candidates based on attributes and criteria they (the search firm) consider desirable for CEOs.

In some instances, executive recruiters serve a dual role. Charan (2005) wrote, "Recruiters must satisfy their clients yet also manage them, helping the search committee to gel so they can extract the criteria they need while keeping requirements broad enough to cast the widest talent net possible" (p. 77). Charan (2005) observed executive search firm criteria consist of: character, vision, team-building, change management, and relationship skills.

There are pitfalls to using executive search firms as well. Wiersema (2002) wrote, "The search firm, lacking direction in identifying the attributes an executive must have to turn the company around, brings in candidates who have been successful in the past but may have no particular knowledge of the company's industry or competitive situation" (p.4). Guy (2001) cautioned on some of the challenges corporate boards may face when retaining executive search firm services such as: insufficient reference checking; minimal comparative evaluation of candidates; presentation of only candidates' strengths; and lack of confidentiality.

Another potential issue with executive search firm participation is around corporate board decision-making. Charan (2005) stated that sometimes the executive search firm selection is flawed. The executive search firm selected may have been a good choice for one company, but may not be a good choice for another. In addition, most boards do not examine search firms' track records – that is, how many CEOs the executive search firm has placed have succeeded or failed. The corporate board of directors committee responsible for retaining an executive search firm must be able to communicate the corporate vision and the CEO selection criteria they expect to meet.

BOARD OF DIRECTOR AND CEO CANDIDATE DEMOGRAPHIC SIMILARITIES

Zajac and Westphal (1996) introduced demographic similarities (in education, functional background, and social networks) between the board of directors and CEO candidates as CEO selection criteria. Zajac and Westphal (1996) revealed that directors favor CEO successors who are demographically similar to themselves (board members) due to psychological and sociopolitical factors.

Al-Alsheikh (2001) wrote, "Using a sample of 232 successions over the period of 1986 to 1991, Zajac and Westphal

(1996) found evidence that directors who possess more power than their CEOs are more likely to select successors who are demographically similar to them" (p. 17). The demographic similarities examined are executive traits listed in the human and social capital theories – knowledge and ability based on schooling, work experience, and social networks (Keiser, 1995). Keiser found successful executives tended to be well educated; and their education backgrounds were from the country's most prestigious schools.

Since 2001, America's confidence in major corporations has diminished. When ethical or legal issues arise that can harm the company's reputation or productivity, the corporate board of directors must recommend what action to be taken to remedy the problem (Richardson, 2004). In some cases, that remedy is the selection of a new CEO. Richardson (2004) pointed out that the role of the corporate board of directors is to represent the interest of shareholders. The board must take into consideration how their decisions and actions in overseeing corporate processes will impact the company's investors. This responsibility also includes CEO selection. Selecting a CEO similar to the existing board's demographics may not necessarily meet the company's needs.

Research Study Results and Themes

The specific population group for this study was corporate board members, HR personnel, and executive search firm professionals involved in criteria for CEO selection. The Sarbanes Oxley Act (2002) recommended limiting the number of corporate boards a board member can be on. The respondents in this study were in compliance with this Act.

Eight themes were identified in this research study. The eight identified themes were: (a) CEO responsibility; (b) leadership skills; (c) expertise; (d) succession planning processes; (e) executive search firm participation; (f) corporate board consensus building; (g) measuring CEO selection success; and (h) technology use and relative importance. The research results are listed below.

THEME 1: CEO RESPONSIBILITY

Two-thirds of research respondents stated the CEO must develop and groom a successor. The corporate board is responsible for protecting shareholders' investments (Walker & LaRocco, 2004). The CEO also protects and enhances shareholder investment through the corporate operations. Shareholders and investment analysts' scrutiny has increased (Rose, 2007). The CEO must meet defined expectations while demonstrating corporate social responsibility.

According to research respondents, grooming a CEO successor is an important criterion for CEO selection. Current CEOs and CEO candidates must be able to develop their successor. It is expected that the CEO will help to select, observe, and nurture key talent being prepared for the CEO role. Although half of the respondents stated the CEO is responsible for grooming a successor, only 16% held the CEO responsible for identifying or naming a successor. One-fourth of the respondents stated protecting shareholder investment is a CEO responsibility.

Theme 2: Leadership Skills

The second observed theme in criteria for CEO selection was leadership. Leadership was depicted as a combination of elements which intertwine personality, group phenomenon, and a social process with a number of people where one person assumes dominance over the others (Bass & Stogdill, 1990, p. 18). Leadership components most expressed in this study were: communication, employee development, integrity, influence, inspiration, and vision.

Two-thirds of the research respondents mentioned employee development as a necessary leadership skill. Half of the respondents mentioned communication as a necessary leadership skill. Leadership integrity has become a growing concern for corporations (Charan, 2005). Fifty eight percent of research respondents recounted their experiences with integrity as CEO selection criteria. Half of the respondents also stated vision and forward-thinking were important.

Theme 3: Expertise

Large corporations focus on pleasing Wall Street (Muller, 2004). CEO candidates' experience and industry knowledge are important to corporate boards for the objective of satisfying the investment community. Corporate boards incorrectly seek charismatic CEO candidates over those with the ability to lead the firm (Khurana, 2002). International experience provides executives with skills that are difficult to acquire domestically. As U.S. firms continue to globalize, international experience becomes more prominent (Magnusson & Boggs, 2006).

The primary CEO experience respondents sought was a background in finance.

Half of the research respondents recounted their experiences with considering CEO candidates with a financial background. Fifty eight percent of respondents stated industry knowledge and business acumen was important. A new CEO will have to be able to lead the corporation through a leadership transition along with a possible change in strategy.

Theme 4: Succession Planning Processes

Succession planning is a process of identifying, developing, and replacing key people over time (Rothwell & Poduch, 2004). Professional and personal development is integrated into the firm's strategic plan (Chartrand, 2005). Succession planning at the CEO level is a process of identifying executives who could assume the CEO role given further development. Half of the research respondents believed their firms had a comprehensive succession planning process in place, and there was an appropriate "C-level" pipeline of candidates to eventually assume the CEO role.

Charan (2005) noted a study conducted by the Corporate Leadership Council where 276 HR executives were surveyed on their firm's succession planning process. Only one fifth of HR executives stated that there was a succession plan in place, and that they were pleased with it. One-fourth of respondents in this study stated their firms had no comprehensive succession planning process in place which supports the existing literature findings.

Theme 5: Executive Search Firm Participation

Executive search firms should be used as an intermediary in the CEO selection process (Khurana, 1998). Whether the search is internal or external, executive search firm involvement may be beneficial. Their experience is vital for coordinating the CEO search, validating candidates' credentials, and providing an accurate comparison of CEO candidate profiles.

Fifty eight percent of research respondents reflected on their experiences in using an executive search firm for CEO selection. One third of research respondents shared experiences of using executive search firms for benchmarking their firm's CEO selection criteria and CEO selection process. One third of research respondents stated executive search firms are not used in their companies due to a strategic initiative and commitment to promoting from within.

Theme 6: Corporate Board Consensus Building

CEO succession events are triggered by inadequate organizational performance (Keiser, 1995). The corporate board must first agree that a CEO change is needed, and the criteria must be defined. In addition, the board must mutually agree on CEO expectations which are communicated to those involved in the CEO selection process (Southerland & Mackey-Ross, 2006). Two thirds of research respondents re-lived experiences with either presenting or being presented a short-list of 3-5 CEO candidates.

CEO candidate discussion occurs. For internal candidates, observation has been on-going during assignments with increased responsibility and authority. For external candidates, executive search firm data and third party referrals are reviewed. Two thirds of respondents emphasized corporate boards were familiar with CEO candidates prior to the candidates being presented. It is rare for a candidate to be presented that does not already have a working relationship or networking affiliation with an existing corporate board member. This familiarity facilitates consensus building in CEO selection.

THEME 7: MEASURING CEO SELECTION SUCCESS

Corporate productivity, corporate valuation, and meeting shareholder expectations are key factors of the firm's performance (King, 2001). Corporate performance expectations factor into CEO selection (Muller, 2004). The expectations used for selecting the CEO are also used in measuring success of the firm and the selected CEO.

Pleasing Wall Street is part of the corporate board's focus (Muller, 2004). Meeting investment community measurements and expectations may be a priority. Forty one percent of research respondents emphasized employee productivity, financial valuation, and investment community expectations as the measuring sticks for assessing CEO selection success. Forty one percent of respondents mentioned the CEO method of interacting with employees (in morale and retention) is also a key, early indicator in measuring CEO success.

THEME 8: TECHNOLOGY USE AND RELATIVE IMPORTANCE

Corporations use technology for gaining a competitive advantage (Day, 2000). The corporation's success and existence may hinge on the effective use of technology (Katz, 2003). Technology expenses are high, and have become a significant part of the corporate budget (Ben-Megachim & Gelbard, 2002).

Three fourths of research respondents acknowledged that technology plays a critical role in their organizations, and 83% acknowledged that corporate operations are dependent upon the effective use of technology. Forty one percent or respondents shared their experiences of how technology use is continuously increasing in their firms. However, none of the research respondents stated technology expertise as criteria for CEO selection.

Corporate CEOs are also corporate board members. Weidenbaum (2003) noted 90% of the time; the CEO serves in a dual role of President of the company and chair of the corporate board of directors. Al-Alsheikh (2001) found CEO candidates' characteristics will be different from the exiting CEO, but will be similar to board members involved in the CEO selection process. In order to execute Nueman's (2003) triangulation strategy and accumulate more detail on criteria for CEO selection, three companies that replaced their CEO between 2000 and 2005 were randomly selected to review criteria for membership to their corporate board of directors.

The criteria for membership to the board of directors were reviewed from corporate websites. The information is public knowledge and accessible for all interested parties to view. The data from the corporate websites provided a comparison, albeit a small comparison, between the existing literature, research participant responses, and real-life, publicly displayed criteria for corporate board member consideration.

All three corporations listed integrity, experience, and a commitment to contribute time to carry out board member duties. Two of the corporations listed professional achievement and judgment (acumen) as board member criteria. These characteristics align with the research study themes of leadership skills (Theme 2), and expertise (Theme 3). One corporation listed education background as board member criteria. One corporation listed "free of conflict of interest" as board member criteria. None of the corporations listed technology experience as board membership criteria, which is consistent with the existing literature and research participant responses. As a result, the criteria for corporate board membership and corporate CEO selection are similar.

The three corporate websites and Dun & Bradstreet's Reference Book (Hoovers) were also analyzed to compare the new CEO's educational and functional background to the background of the corporate board members who appointed the CEO. In all three companies, the corporate board members and CEO had an MBA in their educational background. In all three companies, more than half of the corporate board members had a functional background in financial operations. In all three companies, neither the appointed CEO nor the corporate board members had an information technology education or functional background in information technology operations.

Research Study Findings

According to the research study's results of respondents' experiences, the primary criteria corporate boards seek in CEOs are: the ability to develop/groom a CEO successor; integrity; industry knowledge; and financial expertise. Additional criteria corporate boards seek are: vision; communication skills; business acumen; ability to influence and inspire others; and international experience. Respondents also believed their firms had a comprehensive "C-level" succession planning process in place, and their firms had developed a good "C-level" succession pipeline.

Respondents presented a mixed bag of experiences with executive search firm participation. Corporations committed to promoting from within did not use executive search firms. Corporations that used executive search firms used them to identify external candidates, compare external candidates to internal candidates, or benchmark their CEO selection processes and policies against other corporations. Respondents also stated CEO selection success is measured by employee productivity, corporate financial performance, and investment community reaction.

Finally, 41% of respondents felt technology use and importance is ever-increasing. However, no respondents expressed technology experience as CEO selection criteria. Respondents' experiences pointed to technology as critical, but not criteria for

CEO selection. The CEO must have basic computer literacy. The CEO must also understand how technology can help the company and provide a competitive advantage. Respondents stated that it is not necessary for CEO candidates to be information technology experts.

Chapter 3:
The Trickle Down Effect

Implications for Leadership

I can not overemphasize the importance of selecting top leadership that possesses a high degree of integrity and ethical behavior. The corporation will follow and emulate the behavior and attitudes demonstrated by ethical and credible leadership. Kouzes and Posner (2002) stressed leaders become the model for what the organization stands for by setting the standards and leading by example. Leaders must communicate shared values and be prepared to discuss those values and expectations in the recruitment, selection, and development of others in the organization. If the top level(s) of the organization adhere to a high degree of integrity and ethics in leadership selection, the other levels of the organization will do likewise.

Radtke and Harr (2008) cautioned that chances are the organization, its board, and employees may go on for years with hiring decisions made today. Yet, most managers take a casual approach to the hiring process. Radtke and Harr (2008) suggested organizations should have detailed policies and procedures that state cultural components and clearly address the expectations – of both sides.

Harshman and Harshman (2008) analyzed key characteristics, behaviors, and qualities of highly ethical leaders. In their analysis, they used an ethical behavior model developed by Patrick Merlevede (2005) defined as jobEQ. This model maps leadership behavior from the beginning of an event through the results phase. The model takes into consideration society, community, and organization (considered the "culture"), and work, family, and recreation (considered the "context"). The jobEQ model states that leaders' results are determined by their attitude, values, and competence. The model supported Harshman and Harshman's (2008) study and highlighted a positive correlation between highly ethical leaders and positive business results.

Therefore, it is equally important to select a CEO with integrity and high ethical standards as well as other levels of leadership in the corporation. The CEO may provide the vision and lay out the corporate direction. However, it is the other levels of leadership and management who are accountable for translating the vision into a corporate strategy and converting that strategy into an executable plan.

Research has shown that highly ethical leaders may also be the organization's top performers. There are cases where transactional leaders have demonstrated integrity and highly ethical traits. This typically occurs within a short-term event for the purpose of achieving a current goal without any vision of a long-term, sustained model of stability (Bass, 1990). However, Harshman and Harshman (2008) conveyed five human resources intervention points to help ensure stability, transformational leadership, and sound leadership selection. The five steps are: recruitment; selection; development; evaluation; and succession planning.

Recruitment is crucial to the other four steps in the HR intervention process. The way leadership is defined and assessed lays the foundation. Soliciting potential leadership candidates that meet the corporate vision of leadership is essential. Selection is the exercise of accumulating a pool of candidates with the intelligence, characteristics, and competencies the organization deems necessary to lead. Once selected, the new leader must write a self assessment and profile so an appropriate development strategy can be established. Both the self assessment and development strategy must align with the corporate goals and objectives. The next phase is evaluation. The organization must provide an accurate and honest performance assessment on the leader's performance in meeting the goals and expectations that were set. Note that this assessment not only evaluates if the expected results were achieved, but also how the leader used their knowledge, skills, and ability to meet those expectations. The final step is succession planning. This step identifies the future organization leaders; positions top performers and high potential performers in roles where they can be further developed – and hopefully, start the HR intervention process over again.

Since June 2005, I have taught over 20 college classes in Management and Supervision; Organizational Theory and Behavior; and Research Utilization to approximately 300 adult learners. These students are employees, supervisors, and managers in a wide array of industries. They are a diverse group that covers the spectrum of demographics found in the existing corporate workplace. In each and every class, multiple learners have openly expressed their observations, experiences, and concerns with unethical leadership behavior in their companies. These concerns consistently led to the question of how unethical, incompetent leaders are selected for their positions.

REAL-LIFE LEADERSHIP SELECTION EXAMPLES

According to Rue and Byars (2004), the selection process consists of seeking and attracting qualified candidates for job vacancies, and choosing the best fit from those candidates. Unfortunately, the real-life examples shared by adult learners from their respective work environments paint a different picture. Rue and Byars (2004) also suggested the Peter Principle is still prominent (individuals are selected or rise to the level of their incompetence). Listed below are four examples from adult learners (in very general terms) of inadequate leadership selection:

1. External candidates have been selected who were less qualified than internal candidates;
2. To avoid a lawsuit or non-compliance with the Equal Employment Opportunity Commission (EEOC), non-qualified candidates were selected;
3. To avoid selecting a qualified candidate with different demographics than the existing leadership, the first non-qualified candidate with similar demographics that applied is selected;
4. Totally unqualified friends and relatives are selected for highly visible and critical roles.

The EEOC regulations do not require an employer to hire unqualified employees. The intent of EEO regulations is to ensure all candidates, regardless of demographic makeup, have an equal opportunity at employment. However, research has shown by not employing job candidates in the diverse communities you do business in, is a roadmap to long-term failure.

The most disconcerting behavior I have observed is disregarding the company policies and guidelines for selecting a leader. One example is the job requirement of having a college degree to be considered for a senior leadership position. Another example is the job requirement of having a specified number of years of experience to be considered for a senior leadership position. There are a number of people in leadership positions that do not meet these basic requirements. Once publicized, the management team that participates in this behavior risks losing the trust and confidence of employees.

The following real-life scenarios are research study results and unsolicited examples from students of how selecting the wrong leader (or selecting an unethical leader) can be costly and may undermine the organization's initiatives, reputation, and standing in society. Because of the challenges with managing technological advancements, globalization, and nurturing a diverse workforce in American corporations, these examples inevitably boil down to accepting change in the workplace. The examples particularly touch upon the change in the demographic makeup of American companies, and the disdain for diversity.

Disdain for Diversity

The concept of diversity in the workplace means different things to different people for different reasons. The most common depiction of diversity is based on demographic differences (i.e. age, gender, race, religion, lifestyle, etc.). Diversity can also be depicted by differences in idea generation and business disciplines such as: finance; information technology; marketing, legal, or operations. The following examples will detail leadership behavior with different approaches to managing/leading the American corporate workplace in 2008. The examples address a number of workplace biases, and the consequence of those biased actions.

Disregard for Technological Viewpoints

The corporate, C-level suite's opinion and attitude towards technology leadership appear to be cyclical. As mentioned in Chapter Two, corporate leaders and corporate board members acknowledged the importance of technology to the corporation. Technology provides a competitive advantage; it is used throughout all aspects of corporate activity; and technology "downtime" can adversely impact corporate operations.

However, prior to circa 1996, IT leadership reported to a corporate officer, typically the CFO. From 1997-2000, the concern and uncertainty around technology operations for the Century rollover (known as Y2K) placed technology at the forefront. During this era, the opinions and knowledge of the CIO was highly valued. In some instances, the CIO was escalated to report directly to the CEO. Once Y2K compliance and mitigation activities were complete, the CIO role returned to the earlier role of reporting to the CFO (even though the stakes of technological impact were still high).

This example shows that technology leaders' viewpoints are highly regarded and sought for technology decisions, but not so much for business decisions not involving technology. Thus, corporate C-level leaders including the CEO must be selected who are capable and willing to value these diverse opinions. Oversight or disregard of technology viewpoints could be perilous to organizational survival.

Selection of Technology Leaders

Shore (2005) stated IT leadership affects corporate IT culture, IT strategy, and IT staff commitment. The leadership style of the person selected to lead an IT entity (organization, department, or project) has a significant bearing on the success of that entity. To a large degree, American corporations still believe in rewarding hard workers who are successful in helping the organization meet its goals. Sometimes the reward is monetary. Sometimes the reward is a promotion – with increased responsibility and authority - and subordinates!

Working with others and getting things done through others is a characteristic of successful leaders. In IT, leaders may be successful because of their skills in managing and effectively using technology. Selecting a successful, hard working technology expert to a leadership role of managing people (without developing and training in managing people) can lead to an unproductive and inefficient organization. Managing technology is a science. Consistently applying the same methods will predictably deliver the same results. Managing people is an art. Using one management technique for all employees may not produce the same desired result.

Over the years, I have observed the behaviors, values, and leadership style of successful IT professionals who were selected to lead other IT professionals. In the role of leader, IT professionals did not consistently demonstrate the interpersonal skills or the ability to develop others that is necessary to provide motivation and influence others. As individual contributors, IT professionals were successful in accomplishing their objectives; and as leaders, unreasonably expected subordinates to accomplish objectives in the exact same manner. This is not to say IT leaders are not successful. Once given the appropriate leadership development, they become very successful. However, selecting an IT leader to manage other IT professionals without providing leadership training has proven to fail.

AGE DIVERSITY IN THE WORKPLACE

Roscigno, Mong, Byron, and Tester (2007) conducted a study on age discrimination in employment in the state of Ohio. Their study examined over 12,000 age discrimination cases filed with the Ohio Civil Rights Commission from 1988 to 2003. Roscigno et al (2007) selected 120 of these cases to conduct a more thorough qualitative examination. They found that workers primarily around the age of 50 experienced age discrimination. Manufacturing and construction workers were most often subject to age discrimination. The types of discrimination discovered in the study were termination (66%); harassment (12%); and exclusion from hiring (10%). Some of the excuses used to exclude older workers were inability to fit the company profile, not possessing the necessary competencies, financial costs, personal liabilities, and lack of drive. The study further pointed out that women were discriminated against on both age and gender because companies viewed married women as secondary family earners.

Selecting, or more prominent in today's environment, not selecting a viable leader based on their age is a difficult concept to grasp for four reasons. First, the basic premise of the recruiting, interviewing, and selecting process is to gather a pool of talented, knowledgeable, and competent candidates and select the best one. If workers are omitted because of their age, the talent pool may be incomplete. Second, the vital knowledge transfer process can not be effectively executed if the personnel involved in the process do not have the knowledge. Third, this biased practice is very short-sighted. Do corporations really want to omit and discourage the age group with the most discretionary income from purchasing their products and services? Fourth, the practice defies the golden rule (do unto others…). Regardless of one's other demographics, everyone will age and eventually become a member of the 50 and over age group.

Nonetheless, I have received confirmation from over 15 executive search firms, staffing agencies, and consulting companies that their corporate clients do not want employment candidates over the age of 45. According to Williamson (2008), executive search firms and recruiting agencies are being instructed by their client corporations (implicitly and explicitly) to only present candidates in a certain age group. I have not conducted any research to identify companies whose leadership has placed this demand. However, research has shown that the average age of corporate board members (which typically includes the CEO) is over 50 years old. It may be interesting to know what level of corporate leadership has initiated and supported this demand.

DISCRIMINATION IN LEADERSHIP SELECTION

I have intentionally combined the discussion on leadership selection of protected groups (i.e. women, minorities, and special needs employees) together. Our diverse, multi-cultural, religious, and ethnic beliefs on how we interact with each other – and how we treat each other in America – can not be adequately addressed in this book on leadership selection. The following Harvard Law Review (2008) article was a very good synopsis of the current view of workplace inequality.

According to the Harvard Law Review (2008), most Americans believe they live in a society of meritocracy; everyone has equal opportunity for success regardless of race or sex.

However, the article stated that as of 2005, female executives were making seventy-seven cents for every dollar made by their male counterparts. Equally qualified employees with African American-sounding names have a tougher time obtaining interviews (let alone a job) than employees who do not have African American names.

Between 1999 and 2001, Livers and Carver (2003) surveyed approximately 290 professionals who held different titles, positions, and levels of authority in multiple corporations. They found that even though corporations do not tolerate blatant discrimination, there are subtle signs that corporations remain inhospitable to not only blacks, but other non-traditional leaders. Livers and Carver (2003) also found that organizations benefit from effective leadership by embracing diversity and taking advantage of diverse contributions and insight. Cole (2007) reported that as of 2007, there were 13 female and 4 African American CEOs leading Fortune 500 companies. In my research, I was unable to find one (1) CEO with special needs.

Leading Multi-Cultural Teams

I would be remiss if I did not include a section on my own leadership attitude, behavior, and style in this discussion on the consequences of leadership selection. During my climb up the proverbial corporate ladder in the mid-1990's, I was given the opportunity to select and lead a team of IT and business professionals to transfer the existing Enterprise Resource Planning (ERP) processes to a fully automated system. Those with a project management background can appreciate the ever-so familiar dynamic: too few resources (people and money); too little time; scope change in the middle of the project; assessment of project delivery by senior management.

On this team of 12 highly talented professionals of diverse backgrounds, there were two contractors of the Muslim faith. I knew this because they requested one hour on every Friday to go to the nearby Mosque to pray. I had no qualms about granting their request. I made sure the rest of the team was aware of my decision and how the team would continue to function during that one hour every Friday. Besides, these contractors were very good at their work, and they more than made up for the time in productivity. Furthermore, there were no employee issues or a second thought aired by the team. And yes, our project was delivered on time and under budget.

I believe my inclusive, consensus-building management style and mutual respect for others played a role in my decision-making. I mentioned this scenario occurred prior to September 11, 2001. I had only considered ability to do the job in the selection process. I would like to think my decision would have been the same post 9/11. One can only speculate. Would I have involved my manager? Would other team members have been concerned? Would the project have been completed based on my decision?

Corporate Downsizing –
Chosen to Stay; Chosen to Leave

Downsizing is an accepted part of today's corporate environment. When business is good, companies take on more employees. When business hits a down-turn, employees may be released. Choosing who stays and who goes is just as important as choosing who leads. If the company has poorly selected its leaders, there is little confidence of those leaders successfully choosing who stays in a corporate downsizing. Employees chosen to stay must have the ability to take on more work, and remain productive during a time of transition and possibly, uncertainty.

Chafkin (2007) identified the "final frontier" of human resources: the outsourced termination. HR outsourcing in today's business environment consists of bringing in consultants to terminate employees. This behavior demonstrates leadership inability or unwillingness to do this undesirable task.

In Chapter Two, I discussed the use of technology for selecting leaders. There is now technology and software that can help managers decide whom to fire (Chafkin, 2007). The program starts by asking how many employees are going to be terminated. Employees are then rated on a scale of 1-5, taking into account employee age, race, and union status (to mitigate lawsuit risks). The software can then generate a list of "eligible" employees to terminate; calculate severance pay; cut final paychecks and format termination letters. The application is also data-driven. When executed, it can automatically deactivate key cards and email accounts of the employees being released.

Employee knowledge of such a program will undoubtedly increase their stress level, and subsequently, adversely impact their ability to be productive. Lack of communication and interaction with employees may exacerbate the issue. Consider the scenario where a hard-working employee who has very little contact with their manager comes to work and can not gain access because of a "glitch" with their access card. One of the first reactions would be they were terminated and not informed of the decision. Here are three other examples of poor leadership in handling corporate downsizing.

One, a memo goes out to approximately 500 employees in a division of a large company on a Friday morning. The memo states that all employees should stay close to their phone for a call on Saturday afternoon. Employees will receive a call stating whether they should return to work on the following Monday or if they have been terminated. Two, all 200 employees of a company are summoned to an afternoon meeting to be held in two different rooms. In one room, the employees are told they still have a job and return to work. In the other room, employees are informed (as a group) that they have been terminated. They are instructed to leave immediately and will be allowed to return during the weekend to gather and pack their belongings. Three, in a group of 100 employees, 10% are terminated and publicly escorted out by security.

In all of these examples, there is a financial and social impact to the company. From a financial perspective, the planned expense reduction as a result of the downsizing is offset by the lack of productivity from the remaining employees. There will be more discussion, concern, and fear over the way the terminations were handled for days, maybe even weeks. Return to the scenario above about the "glitch" with the key card, and consider how the anxiety level can escalate exponentially. From a social perspective, word on how the terminations were conducted will get to the other departments, and eventually seep out to the public, to shareholders, to vendors, and the community at large. Whatever the corporate reputation was before, will be compromised.

Chapter 4:
Conclusion

An editorial written in *Pensions & Investments* (2007) suggested corporate boards should not reward departing CEOs who presided over corporate losses of hundreds of millions of dollars in shareholder value. The editorial stated CEOs should understand if they hurt the wealth of the shareholders, the CEOs wealth will suffer as well. The other side of this challenge is that it may become difficult to recruit top CEO talent if such a stipulation is viewed by CEO candidates as unreasonable. Maybe the solution is a consistent flat-rate salary for all corporate CEOs.

Recommendations for Improvement

There are no silver bullets or guarantees of success in selecting corporate leadership. Each organization has a different set of values, beliefs and culture. One size does _not_ fit all. The five recommendations listed here should be considered by organizations that are: committed to effectively using technology; sincerely dedicated to recruiting, developing, and retaining a diverse workforce; and passionate about maintaining ethical leadership behavior within their firms.

The recommendations are focused on executable strategies in the areas of information technology, inclusion, and integrity. Successful adoption of these recommendations may result in significant improvement of employee productivity and organization profitability at a time when investor expectations are high and employee morale and consumer confidence are low. The recommendations are:

1. Include technology expertise on the corporate board of directors;
2. Develop an employee skills database to manage organization workforce levels and analyze employees' knowledge, skills, and abilities needed to accomplish organization goals and objectives;

3. Oversee the performance management and succession planning process with an extremely high level of integrity and lack of bias;

4. Address the organization pipeline. Aggressively invest in the American education system to develop business talent within the U.S. with the same rigor used to offshore business operations;

5. Embrace workplace diversity. Support, reward, and publicly recognize whistleblowers with the moral courage to report unethical behavior that may result in substantial financial damage to the company.

Include Technology Leadership on the Corporate Board

The results of this research study found that information technology is a necessity for corporate operations. Technology is not only used for a competitive advantage, but is also relied upon for daily, routine activities. The first recommendation is for corporate boards to establish a technology committee at the corporate board level (or appoint a board member with technology expertise) if one does not already exist. The corporate board can define the objectives and expectations of the technology role, along with the value added to the firm for its existence.

CEO selection criteria literature revealed analyses of the changing business landscape. However, in today's ever-changing technology based economy, no observed research reported cases of a Chief Information Officer (CIO) appointed to the role of CEO in a non-technology company. It remains a curiosity that technical expertise does not enter into the equation as criteria for CEO selection. Companies use technological advances to gain or maintain a competitive advantage. During the *dot com era*, and the Year 2000 century rollover initiative, CEOs had a place at the corporate decision-making table. Today, information technology, technology security, and technology confidentiality are critical to corporate success (Day et al, 2003).

Dearstyne (2005) stressed information technology is an essential part of the modern-day organization. CIOs are becoming more sophisticated, less wedded to technology, and more encompassing in their missions. Dearstyne (2005) went on to emphasize that business leaders must view IT as a direct contributor and partner in organization growth. IT leaders contribute strategy, insight, high-level planning, and corporate technology security.

Sinnett and Boltin (2006) analyzed the results of a CFO technology issues survey conducted by the Financial Executives Research Foundation. With over 560 CFO responses, technology security scored the highest average rating. Moreover, upgrading and replacing legacy systems was the most frequently rated number one critical technology issue.

Davis, Rath, and Scanion (2004) reported that the average annual IT cash budget in large companies is over $300 million. In addition, corporations' IT budgets are growing at 3.4% a year on average. Mamaghani (2006) found that technological advances have enabled companies to increase operating efficiencies, reduce cost, enhance global presence, improve communications, and work from remote locations. Under CIO leadership, it appears organizations are achieving desired business results and reaping the benefits of solid performance that boards look for from the CEO. Given the same increased responsibility and authority like other C-level executives being "groomed" for the CEO position, the CIO may produce similar positive results.

Develop an Employees' Skills Inventory Database

The second recommendation for corporate improvement is to develop a skills inventory database of the company's most valued asset – its employees. An internal employee skills inventory will facilitate the employee resource planning process. Recruiting, interviewing, and selecting external candidates can be expensive. The expense is even higher when the wrong candidate is selected (Byrne, 1999). There are increased development costs or potential termination and re-selection costs when attempts at developing an underperforming leader do not work.

An employee skills inventory will provide insight into the existing competencies the organization has in-house. The skills inventory will help the organization proactively address gaps in required knowledge, skills, and abilities for completing future initiatives. The organization will have time to address the gaps by providing employee training and development. If necessary, consultants and contractors can be brought in on a temporary basis to fill short-term goals and objectives.

OVERSEE PERFORMANCE MANAGEMENT AND SUCCESSION PLANNING PROCESSES

Recommendation three is to execute sound leadership and guidance over the performance management and succession planning processes. Leaders at all levels of the organization have expressed concern with writing and delivering performance reviews. In my observation and experience, I have found that establishing mutually agreed upon goals at the beginning of the year will make delivering the performance review a lot simpler. Having employees participate in setting their goals for the year has three benefits.

First, the leader has an opportunity to communicate with their employees and share the organizational goals and objectives. Second, research has shown employees are more productive when they are included in decision-making and organization decisions (Bass, 1990; Kouzes & Posner, 2002). Third, employees will have "skin in the game" because they have helped in setting the goals they are expected to achieve.

The succession planning process is an opportunity to identify top performers, and further develop the corporate pipeline with high potential talent which will become the future leadership of the company (Charan et al 2001). A formal process of identifying the organization's existing talent, and monitoring its development should be done at least once, and preferably twice per year. Talent management of valued employees is essential to consistency and continuity of corporate initiatives. Rothwell and Poduch (2004) suggested that succession planning is the activity of making provisions for the development and replacement of key people over time. For companies that follow the practice of promoting from within, the succession planning process will also include executive positions up through the CEO.

From a financial viewpoint, recruiting, interviewing, and selecting external talent is more expensive than grooming internal talent that is already aligned with the organization's shared values, beliefs, and culture. Further, promoting from within is an ideal mechanism for retaining top performers. Talented employees will eventually leave the company if they sense there is no opportunity for growth (Marsh, 2006).

Invest in the American Education System

Recommendation four highlights the infinite opportunity to cultivate American business leaders. High School and College students seek structure and are motivated by opportunity for gainful employment. During the past ten years, our education system has begun to lag behind other countries – especially in the area of technology. Some college students feel technology is not the field to go into. They tend to shy away from technology as their field of study because of the perception that the technology jobs are being shipped offshore.

For those organizations that view contributing to the American education system as part of their corporate social responsibility, I am sure the donations are greatly appreciated. I commend those with the greater foresight who view contributing to the American education system as an investment in their organization's future. Imagine a process where college students and high school seniors are trained as corporate interns in fields such as finance, marketing, and information technology. These interns could develop and maintain the highly recommended employee inventory skills database at a cost very comparable to what is paid for off-shoring the same activity. In addition, such an activity would serve as motivation for students to pursue a degree and potentially work for a company where they have already gained business knowledge.

EMBRACE WORKPLACE DIVERSITY

The fifth and final recommendation for corporate improvement is to make a sincere effort to embrace diversity in the workplace. The statistics reported in chapters one, two, and three of this book do not support the claims of meritocracy in our corporate environment. Nor was their any evidence of a consistent pattern of ethical behavior in selecting leaders.

Acknowledging "whistleblowers" who report unethical behavior is far cheaper than the alternative of mitigating and/or paying thousands of dollars in lawsuit claims. Livers and Carver (2003) noted that workplace tension may occur due to the type of visibility an employee gets, or whether an employee gets high-profile and challenging assignments. Addressing and correcting unethical behavior in leadership selection will retain employee trust, boost consumer confidence, and minimize the potential tension and productivity disruption.

MEASURING SUCCESS

Adhering to the improvement recommendations in this book, or for that matter, any book on leadership may not immediately produce desired results. However, these recommendations will guide the organization down the right path of selecting sound transformational leadership, and reaping the benefits and advantages of the decision. Nonetheless, there are signs from employees, shareholders, and customers which will provide an indication of progress.

The first measurement is employee satisfaction. Corporations conduct employee surveys to gauge employee job satisfaction with the company, their leadership, and their benefits. It is part of human nature to share life's experiences with others (i.e. family, friends, co-workers). Low participation (under 33%) signals low confidence in the organization's leadership. Things do not bode well if the one-third of the organization can not share their experiences, or they have nothing good to say about their place of employment. Employees' perception may range from there is no benefit in participating; to leadership is incapable or unwilling to act on employee issues; to fear of a negative reaction from management for not giving positive survey responses.

Another employee measuring stick is turnover. Closer scrutiny of the organization and leadership practices is needed if employees are voluntarily leaving the company for a "better opportunity" – especially in a poor employment market where there are few opportunities. A lot has been written on McGregor's (1960) concepts of Theory X and Theory Y employees. Generally speaking, if the leader has high expectations of employees, employee productivity will be high. If leader expectations are low, employee productivity will be low. But what happens to employee productivity and morale when leadership's actions, attitudes, and behaviors are unethical?

Quantitative data on leadership selection and the subsequent impacts (i.e. employee turnover; workplace diversity; number of cases filed for workplace violations, etc.) are documented in the HR department. Qualitative data on leadership selection and the subsequent impacts (i.e. harassment; discrimination; unethical behavior, consumer protection violations) are documented in the office of ethics. Despite attempts to prevent corporate wrongdoing, companies are aware that at times both leaders and employees will undertake inappropriate activity. The role of the organization office of ethics is to mitigate and litigate claims against corporate wrongdoing. Vigilantly monitoring HR and office of ethics statistics will provide a rich source of information on leadership impact.

The second measurement of leadership selection success is shareholder reaction. The investment community provides the highly accepted, quantitative measurement of success – corporate stock valuation. The stock market typically has a positive reaction to CEO succession announcements. Rhim et al (2006) emphasized corporate boards frequently respond to downturns in organization performance by replacing the CEO. This move occurs because of increased demand from shareholders for improved management practices and pressure from the general public for increased corporate accountability.

CEO succession announcements imply change. This change also assumes a positive impact on corporate productivity. Corporate boards seek leaders with charisma (Khurana, 2002). Stockholder reaction to a newly announced CEO is very positive.

The final barometer for measuring leadership selection success is the organization's customers. Customer satisfaction surveys are one way of gauging customer loyalty and confidence. However, the most telling indicator of customer satisfaction is repeat customers. A steady, continuous flow of repeat customers over a long period of time for the organization's goods and services is a positive sign. Corporate leadership that demonstrates corporate social responsibility and contributes to the communities they do business in is another positive sign. Utilizing Third World countries for cheap labor is not a reputation that wins the corporation loyal, repeat customers.

The corporate offshore strategy will continue as an area of debate. U.S. corporations that do business in other countries <u>should</u> have employees at all levels of the organization (with similar pay for similar work) in the countries where they do business. However, corporations solely based in the U.S. have engaged in the practice of eliminating U.S. employees and hiring employees in other countries to reduce operating expenses. Yet, these companies still expect unemployed and underemployed U.S. citizens to purchase their goods and services. Companies that practice discrimination (such as the age discrimination example discussed in Chapter Three) risk losing substantial revenue from the part of the population that has discretionary income. All these signs are ways to measure the impact and consequences of leadership selection.

FINAL THOUGHTS

Qualitative, phenomenological research made it possible to get an in-depth view of the experiences and perceptions of those involved in CEO selection. The CEO sets the tone for the values, attitude, and culture of the organization. The behavioral pattern at the C-level in selecting leaders will be emulated at other levels of the organization. The corporate environment is in need of sound leadership and a comprehensive succession planning process to fill the corporate pipeline with future corporate leaders. Globalization, technology, and changes in workplace diversity will require leadership that is adaptable and amenable to change.

The leadership examples reviewed in this book were meant to highlight the financial and social impact as a result of making poor choices in selecting leadership. The examples were not intended to paint a negative view of corporate activity. Poor leadership selection choices do not endear the corporation to employees, shareholders, or customers. Poor leadership selection choices place an additional burden on companies who already struggle with remaining competitive. It also fuels the perceptions of mistrust, and diminishes the consumer level of confidence in the company.

Even with our current economic, financial, and social challenges, the U.S. remains the best and most prosperous country in the world. Much of our prosperity is due to the success of our businesses and the sound leadership that directs their operations. However, we are not perfect. There is always an opportunity to improve. The challenges that lie ahead provide an opportunity for demonstrating sound leadership based on integrity, ethical behavior, inclusion, and technology.

In closing, it should be noted that employees, vendors, customers, and shareholders will continue to vigilantly observe corporate leadership selection. The attitudes and behaviors of those selected to lead will be closely monitored. It is truly a scenario that will be played out and second-guessed across the global business environment. "The whole world is watching."

References

Ahmed, S. (2005). Desired competencies and job duties of non-profit CEOs in relation to the current challenges: Through the lens of CEO's job advertisements. *The Journal of management Development.* 24(10), 913.

Agrawal, A., Knoeber, C. & Tsoulouhas, T. (2006). Are outsiders handicapped in CEO successions? *Journal of Corporate Finance.* 619-644.

Allgood, S. & Farrell, K.A. (2003). The match between CEO and Firm. *The Journal of Business.* 76, 2.

Al-Alsheikh, S. A. (2001). *An exploratory study of leadership succession on founders of publicly held corporations.* The University of Mississippi. Doctoral dissertation. (UMI No. 3040607). Retrieved on July 27, 2007 from ProQuest database.

Auchterlonie, D.L. (2003). How to fix the rotating CEO dilemma: Best practices of turnaround management professionals. *Journal of Private Equity.* 6 (4), 52-57.

Bartlett, N. (2006). CEO succession demands a formal plan. *Credit Union Magazine.* 72 (8) 30.

Bass, B. M. & Stogdill, R. M. (1990). *Handbook of Leadership: Theory, research, and managerial applications.* (3rd ed.). The Free Press. New York.

Behn, B.K., Dawley, D.D., Riley, R. & Yang, Y. (2006). Deaths of CEOs: Are delays in naming successors and insider/outsiders succession associated with subsequent firm performance? *Journal of Managerial Issues.* 18(1), 32.

Ben-Megachim, M. & Gelbard, R. (2002). Integrated IT Management Tool Kit. *Communications of the ACM.* 45(4), 96-102.

Bennis, W. & O'Toole, J. (2000). *Don't Hire the Wrong CEO*. Harvard Business Review. Retrieved on February 28, 2005, from http://web15.epnet.com/resultlist

Biggs, E.L. (2004). CEO Succession Planning: An emerging challenge for boards of directors. *Academy of Management Review*. 18(1), 105-107.

Boyd, C.O. (2001). Phenomenology the method. In P.L. Munhall (Ed.), *Nursing research: A qualitative perspective* (3rd Ed.). Sudbury, MA: Jones and Bartlett.

Brockmann, E. N., Hoffman, J. J. & Dawley, D. D. (2006). A contingency theory of CEO successor choice and post-bankruptcy strategic change. *Journal of managerial Issues*. 18, 2.

Byrne, J. A. (1999). *Boards share the blame when the boss fails*. Business Week, Issue 3661.

Business Roundtable (2002). Principles of corporate governance. Retrieved September 12, 2007 from http://www.businessroundtable.org.

Cannella, A. A. & Shen, W. (2001). So close and yet so far: Promotion versus exit for CEO heirs apparent. *Academy of Management Journal*. 44.

Carver, J. (2003). What continues to be wrong with corporate governance…And how to fix it. *Ivey Business Journal Online.* London: Sep/Oct 2003.

Carver, M. (2004). When a policy governance board hires a new CEO, what are some important do's and don'ts to remember during the hiring process and the new CEO's early weeks? *Leadership.* Volume 2004 Issue 74.

Chafkin, M. (2007). Meet Rebecca. She's here to fire you. *Inc. Magazine.* 29(11), 25-26.

Charan, R. (2005). *Ending the CEO Succession Crisis.* Harvard Business Review. Retrieved February 28, 2005, from http://web15.epnet.com/resultlist

Charan, R., Drotter, S.J., & Noel, J.L. (2001). *The Leadership Pipeline: How to build the leadership-powered company.* San Francisco: Jossey-Bass.

Chartrand, F. (2005). *Workforce in transition. Succession Planning: A tool for integrating emerging leaders in learning organizations.* Royal Roads University, Canada. Retrieved on July 27, 2007 from ProQuest database.

Ciampa, D. (2005). Almost ready: how leaders move up. *Harvard Business Review.* 83, 46-53, 116.

CIO Insight (2006). *Security and risk strategies become integrated.* Ziff Davis Media Inc. Retrieved on June 24, 2006 from EBSCOhost database.

Coldwell, D.A. (2007). Is research that is both causally adequate and adequate on the level of meaning possible or necessary in business research? A critical analysis of some methodological alternatives. *The Electronic Journal of Business Research Methods.* 5(1), 1-10.

Cole, Y. (2007). *Why are so few CEOs people of color and women?* Diversity Inc. Retrieved October 10, 2008 from http://www. diversityinc.com/public/2696.cfm.

Cone, J.D. & Foster, S.L. (2006). *Dissertations and theses from start to finish: Psychology and related fields.* (2nd ed.). Washington, D.C: American Psychological Association.

Corporate Social Responsibility News (2008). Retrieved October 1, 2008 from http://www.cswire.com/profile/649.html

Creswell, J. W. (2003). *Educational research: Planning, conducting, and evaluating quantitative and qualitative research.* (2nd ed.). Merrill Prentice-Hall. Upper Saddle River, NJ.

Curry, S. R. (2005). Getting your bench right. *Chief Executive.* 212, 30.

Dahya, J. & McConnell, J.J. (2003). Outside Directors and Corporate Board Decisions. Baruch College, CUNY.

Daily, C.M. & Dalton, D.R. (2003). Dollars and sense: The path to board independence. *The Journal of Business Strategy.* 24(3), 41.

Datta, D.K., Guthrie, P. & Rajagopalan, N (2002). Different industries, different CEOs? A Study of CEO career specialization. *Human Resource Planning.* 25, 14-25.

Davidson, W. N., Nemec, C. & Worrell, D. L. (2001). Succession planning vs. agency theory: A test of Harris and Helfat's interpretation of plurality announcement market return. *Journal of Management and Governance.* 6, 4.

Davidson, W. N., Nemec, C., Worrell, D. L. & Lin, J. (2002). Industrial origin of CEOs in outside succession: Board preference and stockholder reaction. *Strategic Management Journal.* 22.

Davidson, W.N, Shengui, T., Worrell, D.L. & Rowe, W. (2006). Ignoring rules of succession: How the board reacts to CEO illness announcements. *Journal of Business Strategies.* 23(2), 93-113.

Davis, K.B., Rath, A.S. & Scanion, B.L. (2004). How IT spending is changing. *McKinsey Quarterly.* Special Edition. P. 58-67.

Day, G. S., Gunther, R. E. & Schoemaker, P. J. (2003). *Wharton on managing emerging technologies.* New York: John Wiley and Sons.

Dearstyne, B.W. (2005). The information enterprise; new challenges new dimensions. *Information Management Journal.* 39(4), 38-45.

Donaldson, W.H. (2003). Corporate Governance. *Business Economics.* 38(3), 16

English, K. (2003). The changing landscape of leadership. *Research Technology Management.* Jul/Aug 2003; 46, 4.

Etchegary, J. (2006). *Research Methods.* Class Lecture. University of Phoenix. RES/721.

Farrell, K. & Whidbee, D. (2002). Monitoring by the financial press and forced CEO turnover. *Journal of Banking and Finance.* 26(12): 2249.

Fisman, R., Khurana, R. & Rhodes-Kropf, M. (2006). Governance and CEO turnover: Do something or do the right thing? *Working Papers.* Harvard Business School.

Ford, R., Boss, R.W.& Angemeier, I. (2004). Adapting to change in healthcare: Aligning strategic intent and operational capacity. *Hospital Topics.* 82(4), 20-29.

Fortune – America's Most Admired Companies (2006). *Fortune Magazine.* Retrieved September 30, 2008, from http://money.cnn.com/magazines/fortune/mostadmired/industries/industry_3.html

Fox, A. (2008). Prune Employees Carefully. *HR Magazine.* 53(4), 66-70.

Fulmer, R.M. & Conger, J.A. (2004). Developing leaders with 2020 vision. *Financial Executive.* 20(5), 38-41.

Garman, A.N. & Glawe, J. (2004). Succession planning. *Consulting Psychology Journal.* 56(2), 119-128.

Graziano, C. & Luporini, A. (2003). Board efficiency and internal corporate control mechanisms. *Journal of Economics & Management Strategy.* 12(4), 495-530.

Groenewald, T. (2004). A phenomenological research design illustrated. *International Journal of Qualitative Methods,* 3(1). Article 4. Retrieved December 6, 2007 from http://www.ualberta.ca/~iiqm/backissues/3_1pdf/groenewald.pdf

Groysberg, B., Nanda, A. & Nohria, N. (2004). *The risky business of hiring stars.* Harvard Business Review.

Guy, C.W. (2001). Eroding ethics of executive search. *Consulting to Management.* Burlingame. 12(3), 51-56.

Hadlock, C. J., Lee, D. S. & Parrino, R. (2002). Chief Executive Officer careers in regulated environments: Evidence from electric and gas utilities.45, 535 – 563.

Harshman, C.L. & Harshman, E. F. (2008). The Gordian Knot of Ethics: Understanding leadership effectiveness and ethical behavior. *Journal of Business Ethics.* 78:175-192.

Hermalin, B.E. (2005). Trends in corporate governance. *The Journal of Finance*. 60 (5), 2351.

Herrity, A. C. (2002). Explaining institutional change: Erosion of the rule for choosing CEOs at United States industrial corporations, 1975 – 1994. Doctoral dissertation, Department of Sociology. University of California, Riverside. *Dissertation Abstracts, International 63/08*. (UMI No. 3061575).

Hiring, Firing CEOs. (2007). *Pensions & Investments*. 35(24), 10.

Hoffman, J.J., Schniederjans, M.J. & Sebora, T.C. (2004). A multi-objective approach to CEO selection. *Infor Journal*. 24(4), 237 – 255.

Hollenbeck, G.P. (2002). Room at the top for wise choices. *In Focus*. 22.

Hoovers. A D&B Company (n.d.). Retrieved January 14, 2008 from http://www.hoovers.com/free/

Hunte-Cox, D. E. (2004). Executive succession planning and the organizational learning capacity. George Washington University. Doctoral Dissertation. (UMI No. 3111403). Retrieved on February 27, 2007 from ProQuest database.

Ives, K.S. (2004). Computer mediation experiences by language-and-culturally diverse global teams. Doctoral dissertation University of Phoenix. *Dissertation Abstracts, International 65/09.* (UMI No. 3144873)

Jentner, D. & Kanaan, F (2006). CEO turnover and relative performance evaluation. MIT Sloan School of Management.

Jones, D. (2003, December 3). "Boomerang CEOs": back on top. *USA Today.* pp. B3.

Jones, D. (2006, July 12). Turnover for CEOs is on record pace: Williams-Sonoma brings back ex-CEO. *USA Today.* pp. B1.

Jones, G.R. (2007). *Introduction to business: How companies create value for people.* New York, NY: McGraw-Hill/Irwin.

Kaplan, A. S. (2006). *Climbing the ladder to CEO Part II: Leadership and business acumen.* (March/April). The Physician Executive. 32(2), 48-49.

Kaplan, A. S. (2006). Climbing the ladder to CEO Part III: Following your own path. (May/June). *The Physician Executive.* 32(2), 16-19.

Katz, R. (2003). *The human side of managing technological innovation* (2nd ed.). New York: Oxford University Press.

Keiser, J. D. (1995). CEO selection from an institutional perspective: A longitudinal research study determining changes in chief executive profiles and labor markets. Doctoral dissertation, Department of Business Administration. University of Illinois at Urbana-Champaign. *Dissertation Abstracts, International 57/04.* (UMI No. 9624383).

Kesler, G.C. (2002). Why the leadership bench never gets deeper: Ten insights about executive talent development. *Human Resource Planning.* 25(1), 32-44.

Khurana, R. (1998). The changing of the guard: Causes, process and consequences of CEO turnover. Doctoral dissertation, Department of Business and Organizational Behavior. Harvard University. *Dissertation Abstracts, International 59/05.* (UMI No. 9832414).

Khurana, R. & Nohria, N. (2000). The performance consequences of CEO turnover. Working paper. Cambridge, Mass.: MIT.

Khurana, R. (2001). Finding the right CEO: Why boards often make poor choices. *MIT Sloan Management Review.* 43(1), 91-95.

Khurana, R. (2002). *Searching for a Corporate Savior: The irrational quest for charismatic CEOs.* Princeton University Press: Princeton, NJ.

Khurana, R, (2002). "The curse of the superstar CEO." *Harvard Business Review.* 80(9), 60-66.

King, P. J. (2001). Crossover chief executives: A hermeneutic approach for leadership selection. Doctoral dissertation. University of San Francisco. *Dissertation Abstracts, International* 62/02. (UMI No. 3005128).

King, W. B. (2005). Who's on Deck? *Bank Director.* 15, 4.

Kouzes, J.M. & Posner, B.Z. (2002). *Leadership: The challenge.* (3rd ed.). San Francisco: Jossey-Bass.

Kwak, M. (2002). Comparing the performance of external successors. *MIT Sloan Management Review.* 43(4), 9-10.

Latham, J. & Vinyard, J. (2004). Baldrige user's guide: Organization diagnosis, design, and transformation. New York: Wiley

Leedy, P.D. & Ormrod, J.E. (2001). Practical research planning and design (7th ed.). Upper Saddle River, NJ: Merrill Prentice Hall.

Livers, A.B., & Carver, K.A. (2003). *Leading in Black and White: Working across the racial divide in Corporate America.* San Francisco: Jossey-Bass.

Maccoby, M. (2004). Why people follow the leader: the power of transference. *Harvard Business Review.* 82(9):76-85, 136.

Maccoby, M. (2005). Creating Moral Organizations. *Research Technology Management.* 48(1), 59.

Magnusson, P. & Boggs, D. J. (2006). International experience and CEO selection: An empirical study. *Journal of International Management.* 12, 107-125.

Mamaghani, F. (2006). Impact of information technology on the workforce of thefuture: An analysis. *International Journal of Management.* 23(4), 845–850.

Marsh, A. (2006). Why companies overlook their own talent hiring outsider CEOscan be a big mistake—and is often a symptom of even bigger problems. *Business 2.0.* San Francisco (June). 7(5), 52.

McCarthy, J.C. (2002, November). *3.3 million U.S. service jobs to go offshore: TechStrategy research brief.* Cambridge, MA: Forrester Research.

McGregor, D. (1960). *The Human Side of Enterprise.* New York, NY: McGraw-Hill.

Merlevede, P.E. (2005). *Moving metaprograms beyond the flatland.* (jobEQ, Lemebeke, Belgium).

Moustakas, C. (1994). *Phenomenological research methods.* Thousand Oaks, CA: Sage.

Muller, R. (2004). Time, narrative and organizational culture: A corporateperspective. *Tamara: Journal of Critical Postmodern Organization Science.* 3(1).

Murphy, K.J. & Zabojnik, J. (2004). CEO pay and appointments: A market-based explanation for recent trends. *American Economic Review.* 94(2).

Naveen, L. (2006). Organizational complexity and succession planning. *Journal of Financial and Quantitative Analysis.* 41(3).

Neuman, W.L. (2003). *Social research methods.* (5th ed.). Upper Saddle River, NJ: Prentice Hall.

Nielsen, J.S. (2004). *The Myth of Leadership: Creating leaderless organizations.* Palo Alto, CA: Davies-Black Publishing.

Ocasio, W. (1999). Institutionalized action and corporate governance: The reliance on rules of CEO succession. *Administrative Science Quarterly.* 44, 2.

Patton, M.Q. (2002). *Qualitative Research & Evaluation Methods.* (3rd ed.). London: Sage.

Paul, J., Costley, D.L., Howell, J.P. & Dorfman, P.W. (2002). The mutability of charisma in leadership research. *Management Decision.* 40(1), 192-200.

Plitch, P. (2003, May). CEO turnover declines in US amid global rise. *Wall Street Journal. pp.* B3.

Pomeroy, A. (2006). Failing at succession planning. *HR magazine.* 51(7), 14.

Qing, C., Maruping, L.M. & Takeuchi, R. (2006). Disentangling the effects of CEO turnover and succession on organizational capabilities: A social network perspective. *Organization Science.* 17(5), 563-576.

Radtke, D. & Harr, L. (2008). Hire smart, reap rewards. *Credit Union Magazine.* 74(6), 24-25.

Rhim, J., Peluchette, J. & Inam, S. (2006). Stock market reactions and firm performance surrounding CEO succession: Antecedents of succession and successor origin. *Mid-American Journal of Business.* 21, 1.

Richardson, J.E (2004). *Annual Editions: Business ethics* (16th ed.). Dubuque, IA: McGraw-Hill/Duskin.

Roscigno, V.J., Mong, S., Byron, R., & Tester, G. (2007). Age discrimination, social closure and employment. *Social Forces,* 86(1), 313-314.

Rose, J. (2007). Corporate directors and social responsibility Ethics versus shareholder value. *Journal of Business Ethics.* 73(3), 319-331.

Rothwell, W. J. & Poduch, S. (2004). Introducing technical (not managerial) succession planning. *Public Personnel Management.* 33(4), 405-419.

Rue, L.W., and Byars, L.L. (2004). *Supervision: Key Link to Productivity.* (8ᵗʰ ed.). New York: McGraw-Hill Irwin.

Rue, L.W., and Byars, L.L. (2007). *Management: Skills and Application.* (12ᵗʰ ed.). New York: McGraw-Hill Irwin.

Santora, J. C. (2004). Passing the baton. Does CEO relay succession work best? *Academy of Management Journal.* 18(4), 157-159.

Sarbanes-Oxley Act of 2002, H.R. 3763, 107h Cong. (2002).

Sebora, T.C. & Kesner, I.F. (1994). The CEO selection decision process: Bounded rationality and decision component ordering. *Journal of Multi-Criteria Decision Analysis.* 5, 183-194.

Sebora, T.C. (1996). CEO-board relationship evaluation. An exploratory investigation of the influence of base rate factors. *Journal of Managerial Issues.* 8 (spring): 54-77.

Sessa, V. (2001). *Choosing a CEO? Don't take the shortcuts.* Business Week1/15/2001.

Shaw, L. E. (2005). Board responsibility for CEO Succession Planning. *Insights: the Corporate & Securities Law Advisor.* May 2005: 19, 5; ABI/INFORM Global

Shen, W. & Cannella, Jr., A.A. (2003). Will succession planning increase shareholder wealth? Evidence from investor reactions to relay CEO successions. *Strategic Management Journal.* 24, 191-198.

Shore, B. (2005). Failure rates in global IS projects and the leadership challenge. *Journal of Global Information.* Technology Management. 8(3), 1-5.

Sinnett, WM. & Boltin, G. (2006). IT Security, Investment top CFO concerns. *Financial Executive.* 22(5), 42-44.

Southerland, K. & Mackey-Ross, C. (2006). Back to basics: How to recruit your next CEO. *Trustee.* 59(8), 15.

Spoolman, S. (2005). Plan now for the next CEO. *Credit Union Magazine.* 71(6), 30.

Stevens, C.D. & Ash, R.A. (2001). "Selecting employees for fit: Personality and preferred managerial style." *Journal of Managerial Issues.* 12, 500-517.

Swain, J. & Turpin, W. (2005). The new world of CEO succession. *Ivey Business Journal Online.* London: Sep/Oct 2005, P.1.

Takeda, M.B., Helms, M.M., Klintworth, P. & Sompayrac (2005). Hair Colour Stereotyping and CEO selection: Can you name any blonde CEOs? *Equal Opportunities International.* 24(1), 1-13.

Thompson, D. W. & Thompson, N. N. (2003). The art of interviewing your next CEO. *Trustee.* 56(20), 14.

Townsend, B. (1996). Room at the top for women. *American Demographics.* Ithaca. 18(7), 28.

Totty, P. (2006). Tools of the trade: look under all the rocks before selecting a candidate. *Credit Union Magazine.*

Trading Action for Access: The Myth of Meritocracy and the failure to remedy structural discrimination. *Harvard Law Review.* June 2008, 121(8), 2156-2177.

Trochim, W.K. (2006). Research methods knowledge base: Qualitative approaches. Retrieved October 21, 2007 from: http://www.socialresearchmethods.net/kb/qualapp.php

Tsoulouhas, T., Knoeber, C. & Agrawal, A. (2007). Contests to become CEO: Incentives, selection and handicaps. *Economic Theory*. 30, 195-221

Turner, F. (2005). *Fundamental Principles of Sound Research*. Class Lecture. University of Phoenix. RES/711.

Vancil, R.F. (1987). A look at CEO succession. *Harvard Business Review*. 65(2), 107.

Walker, J. W. & LaRocco, J. M. (2004). *Succession management and the board*. The Corporate Board. Vanguard Publications.

Wallin, D., Cameron, D.W. & Sharples, K. (2006). Succession planning and targeted leadership development. *Community College Journal*, 76(1), 24.

Weidenbaum, M. (2003). Restoring public confidence in American business. *Washington Quarterly*. 26(1), 53-62.

Wiersema, M. (2002). Holes at the top: Why CEO firings backfire. *Directorship*. Westport: Apr 2003. 29(4), 5.

Williamson, M. (2008). Prejudi-shh... *Accountancy*. 142(1379), 62.

Zajac, E.J. & Westphal, J.D. (1996). "Who shall succeed? How CEO/board preferences and power affect the choice of new CEOs," *Academy of Management Journal,* 29, 1996, 64.

Zhang, Y. & Rajagopalan, N. (2003). Explaining New CEO Origin: Firm versus industry antecedents. *Academy of Management Journal.* 46(3), 327-338.

Zhang, Y. (2001). Three empirical essays on CEO succession: Multi-theoretic perspectives. Doctoral dissertation, Department of Management and Organization. University of Southern California. *Dissertation Abstracts, International 63/05.* (UMI No. 3054830).

Appendix A:
Qualitative Research Study
Interview Questions

Participant ID Number: _____ Date: _____

This is a confidential research study. No other identification is needed

1. Age (optional)
2. Gender
3. Education
4. Functional Background
5. Social Network Affiliations
6. Geographic Location
7. Current Role

8. Length of time as a corporate board member
9. Length of time as a CEO
10. Experience in CEO selection
11. What role does technology play in your company?
12. What are the criteria for CEO selection?
13. Experience in developing CEO selection criteria
14. Describe the desired characteristics of the next CEO in relation to the last CEO
15. Describe what constitutes CEO selection success
16. Describe the firm's succession planning process
17. How does the company develop a pipeline of potential CEO successors?
18. Describe Search Firm participation in CEO selection
19. Describe the steps in the CEO selection process
20. Describe the technology competencies looked for in a CEO candidates

Glossary Of Terms

Boomerang CEO. A boomerang CEO is a retired CEO who comes out of retirement and returns to run their prior company. Companies that have encountered a financial or ethical challenge, or lack a comprehensive succession planning process to identify viable CEO candidates have brought back past CEOs to lead their corporate operations. The objective of bringing back a CEO is to regain the luster and successful performance the company once realized (Jones, 2003).

Business Roundtable. The Business Roundtable is an association of Chief Executive Officers of leading U.S. companies with $4.5 trillion in annual revenues and more than 10 million employees. Member companies comprise nearly one-third of the total value of the U.S. stock markets and represent over 40% of all corporate income taxes paid. Collectively, they returned $112 billion in dividends to shareholders and the economy (Business Roundtable, 2002).

"C Level" Officer. C-Lever Officers are corporate executives who report directly to the CEO. For example, Chief Finance Officer, Chief Marketing Officer, and Chief Operating Officer are senior leaders who are typically found on the Chief Executive Officer's leadership team (Curry, 2005).

CEO dismissal. CEO dismissal is when a CEO is fired, forced out, retired, or resigned. CEO dismissals may be voluntary or involuntary (Fisman et al, 2006).

Crossover CEO. A Crossover CEO is a leader who came into the company from another industry (King, 2001). As an example, a CEO from a manufacturing firm being appointed CEO of a technology firm would be considered a crossover CEO.

Horse race succession. Horse race succession occurs when insider CEO Candidates are identified and pitted against each other. Candidates are informed that they are being groomed for the CEO position. Whoever performs the best over a specified period of time will be chosen. Horse race succession may conclude without a winner, in which case the process starts over. Selection criteria to judge the candidates often shift during the race (Vancil, 1987).

Interim CEO. An Interim CEO is a leader who is brought in to implement strategic initiatives while existing core management teams, faced with short-term shareholder pressures, continue to focus on day-to-day operations (Ford, Boss & Angemeier, 2004)

Outside CEO. A CEO who has been with the organization for less than one year (Khurana, 1998)

Particular information. Particular information is information that can only be gathered as a consequence of direct experience and observation. Particular information consists of detailed information on the attributes, character, idiosyncrasies, and accomplishments of an individual as opposed to simple general information, such as work history and education credentials (Khurana, 1998)

Relay succession. Relay succession is an anticipated change where CEO announces their intention to step down from their position at some future date and a successor has been identified; groomed and appointed/promoted to CEO (Rhim et al, 2006; Santora, 2004; Shen & Cannella, 2003). The exiting CEO and the heir apparent work jointly during the interim period until leadership passes from one CEO to the next (Zhang & Rajagopalan, 2003).

Index